"We are all apprentices in a craft no one ever becomes a master."
—Ernest Hemingway

Also by Mark Teppo

Jumpstart Your Novel

Silence of Angels
Solitaire
The Potemkin Mosaic
Rudolph! He Is the Reason for the Season
The Court of Lies (collection)
Earth Thirst
Heartland
Lightbreaker

THE FOREWORLD SAGA

The Mongoliad (co-authored with Erik Bear, Greg Bear, Joseph Brassey, Nicole Galland, Cooper Moo, & Neal Stephenson)
Katabasis (co-authored with Joseph Brassey, Cooper Moo, & Angus Trim)

The Lion in Chains (co-authored with Angus Trim)
Cimarronin (co-authored with Ellis Amdur, Charles C. Mann, & Neal Stephenson)

Sinner
Dreamer
Seer
The Beast of Calatrava

FINISH YOUR NOVEL!

a writer productivity guide by **MARK TEPPO**

TEPPOBOX

Finish Your Novel! is a practical how-to guide that presents one author's view on the craft of writing. The views expressed herein are his and his alone. Portions of this book were previously published as *Planning, Plotting, and Progress*.

Copyright © 2018 Mark Teppo

All rights reserved, which means that no portion of this publication may be reproduced or transmitted, in any form or by any means, without the express written permission of the author.

This book was printed in the United States of America. It is a TEPPOBOX publication, which falls under the aegis of Firebird Creative (Clackamas, OR).

Making the words happen!

Square illustrations by Neal Von Flue.

First TEPPOBOX edition: August 2018.

www.teppobox.com

FINISH YOUR NOVEL!

"There is only one plot—things are not what they seem."
—Jim Thompson

TABLE OF CONTENTS

INTRODUCTION
Let's Talk about Writing 1

PART ONE: PLANNING
In the Beginning 9
Permission 16
Productivity 25
Space 34
Glorious Writing Time 38

PART TWO: TALKING ABOUT STRUCTURE
Planting Seeds 47
Topiary Action 54
Connecting Plot Dots 58
Character 64
Chewing on the Scenery 69
Pruning 77

PART THREE: STAYING THE COURSE
The Late Night Pep Talk 83
Pareto's Secret 88
Reaching the End 93
Octopodes 99
Exeunt 102

APPENDIX A: EXTRA READING 107
APPENDIX B: CHARTS & BOXES & STUFF 110

ACKNOWLEDGMENTS 119
ABOUT THE AUTHOR 120

LET'S TALK ABOUT WRITING

Writing is hard.

Let's just say that up front, because it's a large part of why we're all here. There's an old saying that "authors" are people who "like to have written," and "writers" are people who "are writing." Writing is, like any other profession, a job that you only get better at by doing. Some have innate talent, which gives them a jump on the rest of us, but mostly, it's dull, dreary work of getting your butt in the chair and yanking words out of your brain.

Every November, there's a national frenzy called NaNoWriMo,[1] which is a lovely group excuse to put aside everything else and go write. Lovely for the thirty days that is November, but what happens on the first of December? Or the eighth of May? Or any other day of the year? There's all kind of life stuff going on, isn't there? Stuff that gives you an excuse not to write, because—let's be honest with ourselves here—writing probably isn't your

---

[1] National Novel Writing Month. It started as an excuse for a half-dozen people to get together and give each other grief about not writing, and has turned into an actual "job" for some people. Crazy how that works.

main revenue stream. Writing is something you yearn to do—something that speaks to a quivering bit of your soul. Something that you tell yourself you have to do or you'll go bonkers.

If that is what writing is for you, then you are not alone with your frustration and panic. Writing takes time, and time is a commodity that always seems to be in deficit.

What is that John Creasy says in Tony Scott's *Man on Fire*? "I wish . . . I wish you had more time."

Fortunately, none of us are facing Victor Fuentes's fate, but still, the wish remains.

I get that writing is hard. I really do. There's never enough time. There's never enough quiet head space to do what you need to do in order to write your book. And it's going to be like this for years while you do your time in these nasty trenches of the early days on the road to publication. Someday, the sky will open and angels will descend, bearing the magical certificate that says you have permission from the Universe to give that soul-sucking day job the middle finger and stay home and write full time. And it will be a glorious day, amen. But even then, you'll discover a whole new realm of time-suckers, attention-stealers, and writing obstacles that will keep you from your writing time. Leveling up doesn't make things easier, per se; it just means the obstacles and stressors are different.

This is true of any job, really. You go from working the fryer to microwaving burgers to pushing buttons on the shake machine, and each one of those jobs seems cooler and easier from the other side of the kitchen, but when you get there, you discover they've got their own quirks, which makes *that* job suck. Even when you get away from the back of the kitchen, there's the whole 'talking to people' thing about working working the front counter. It never gets easier.

This is supposed to be a pep talk, by the way. A quick-chat intro meant to rev you up. Let's get ready to take on the challenge of finishing that book, right? We're going to solve every problem and launch ourselves into the stratosphere.

The honest secret is that writing is work, and you have to treat it as such. You have to show up—every day—and put in your hours. If there is no time in the day to put in "hours," then you have to put in minutes. Ten. Fifteen. Twenty. Thirty. Whatever you can get. You have to start somewhere, and you have to keep doing it.

I've been putting off writing the first part of this book for months, citing the myriad of *more important* things that are on my plate. *I'll get to it tomorrow* has been my daily refrain, and when tomorrow arrives, I say it again. And if you do that too often, *I'll get to it tomorrow* becomes the rule. It becomes your mantra. Your guiding principle. Your default answer.

I'll get to it tomorrow.

I don't want that carved on my tombstone, frankly. Nor do I want *I wish I had spent more time writing* there either. I'll make you a deal. Right here and now. Let's put aside all the excuses and call ourselves "writers." And then we'll follow through and do the work.

Now, if you haven't started your book, you should go off and do that. At the very least, you might want to grab a copy of *Jumpstart Your Novel*—the predecessor to this book—and do the whole Nine Box Outline exercise that can be found in that book.[2] A lot of this book doesn't work all that well if you haven't started writing, and so I'm going to assume that writing the book isn't why you're here. It's not writing that is getting in the way.

If you are a) you're stuck, or b) you can't fathom how to find the time to write, or c) you enjoy watching a middle-aged man perform cheap circus tricks and make balloon animals, then this book is for you. Though, that whole thing about making balloon animals is more metaphor than actual tradecraft. Sorry.

What are we going to do here? Well, we're going to do some talking about writing, and then we're going do some plotting—the world domination kind—and then we'll talk about making structure and keeping motivated.

We'll spend some time talking about the early stages of writing: organizing your thoughts, building an outline, getting the right beverage (hot or cold), making sure your favorite chair conforms properly to your butt, and finding time to write.

---

[2] Shameless plug aside, this is also a warning that I'm going to use some of the lingo and methods from that book under the assumption that you have a passing familiarity with what I'm talking about. So, you know, variable mileage, *caveat elixir*, *don't take your eyes off the donkey,* and all that.

And we'll answer the burning questions of all time: How does that outline turn into thousands of words of sparkly prose? How do we get our characters to behave long enough for the story to sweep them away? How do we make a functional plot? How do we make sure we know what we're doing as we write this book?

And once we know these answers, we're going to take your cocktail-napkin scrawl of an idea, blend it up with all those stacks of loose paper filled with illegible "plotting" notes, and burn on through to the last page of your manuscript where you get to type the words "THE END."

Then it will be time to celebrate with a strong cocktail and a bout of running naked down the street, screaming, "I am an AUTHOR."

Er, or not. How you celebrate is really up to you.[3]

---

[3] Anthony Trollope, who wrote nearly fifty books that were the delight of his generation, never stopped being a "writer." He had an inviolate block of time—three hours a day—where he wrote. If he finished a novel during that block—and no, he didn't start that same novel at the beginning of that block—he would immediately take down a blank sheet of paper and start the next book. So, while there is a great deal of value in rewarding yourself for finishing a project, let's not lose the momentum you've finally built up. Once only have I been smart enough to do this, and oh goodness goodness goodness, I wish I had the wherewithal to do this every time.

PART ONE

PLANNING

IN THE BEGINNING

It's easy to talk about writing a book. It's easy to talk about the outlining and the scope and 'oh so many wonderful ideas' part. But the actual writing—the physical act of sitting down and doing the time to get those words out of your head and onto the page—that can be an absolute slog. It can take weeks, months—years, even—and no one cares about the book in the slightest during this time. Why? Because it's not a thing yet. A real thingie thing. Not an imaginary thing. Our heads are full of imaginary things, right? All the things. All day long.

But you have to figure out how to take all those thoughts and ideas and fun explody bits whirling around non-stop in your head and get them down on the page. You have to fix them in place. Go all lepidopterist on them. Only then does the idea become real.

Look. You know this. You can sit for hours, staring at the blank page, being utterly aware of nothing else. The book doesn't write itself. It's waiting for you to finish your chores or run out of excuses as to why you're not sitting in that chair. It's waiting patiently for you get out of your own damn way and write. The book will nod patiently and understandingly when you tell it that you're just not feeling "in the mood" today. *That's okay,* the book will say, *I'll be here tomorrow.* And it will be.

But tomorrow? Oh, there's a whiff of failure about it, isn't there? A stink that—*wait, do I need to take out the garbage? I definitely need to take out the garbage, and oh, geez, I should wipe down the counters in the kitchen too while I'm here. And gosh! There's no food in the refrigerator; I should go shopping. And while I'm out grocery shopping I should . . .*

Meanwhile, the book sits and waits. Eventually, though, it will get bored. It'll yawn, play with a dust bunny for a bit, and then then it will wander off. See? It's totally the book's fault. *It* wandered off. You were just taking care of other chores. Important things that needed doing, right?

None of it was writing, though.

Now, if there was a merit badge for "Dodging Writing," I'd have one. Not only can I spell "procrastinator," I can play one on and off TV. I could even teach a graduate level seminar course on "Dissembling and Other Tactics For Avoiding Creative Work." You'd be graded on how well you put off actually getting anything done. Of course, I wouldn't have a syllabus, but whatever, I'll get to it eventually. We all know the coursework.

I've spent a lot of hours not writing. I've even spent some of those hours thinking about why I've not been writing. Occasionally, I pretend all that thinking is actually writing, but such nonsense only last for a few minutes. Alas.

Granted, I've gotten a lot of other stuff done during these times, which helped my self-esteem and kept my house from collapsing on me. But I wasn't making words. Eventually, I even admitted out loud that I didn't like writing—a bummer to hear, and probably true—and that sent me into a sprawling funk, a funk that I finally realized was the Best Excuse Yet.

Recently, a friend mentioned he was trying to finish a book, and the secret of his success was peer pressure. He had several pals stand fast and say: "Yes, we will be your witnesses. Finish the damn book or owe us." That's a fine challenge, and I thought: *Well, hell, I can do that.*

"I want in," I told my friend. "I want some of that peer pressure fear too."

Never mind that I was barely a third of the way into the draft of the novel. That wasn't important. What mattered was me telling myself that—for a week—everything else was secondary to writing. No social media. No fretting about writing newsletters or blogging. No marketing copy. No publishing business. No book layout or cover design work. Just writing. It was like going on vacation, except I would be hiding in my office. And you know what? I wrote 4,000 words the next day. Just like that. *Bam!*

The following day, I wrote less than a hundred, and not for a lack of trying. That burst of activity made me realize that the book lacked focus. It'd been hanging around for months—caught on my neck like that albatross of old—and the main reason it wasn't going anywhere was because I didn't know why I was writing it.

I didn't know what character growth I wanted to accomplish. I didn't know what the protagonist wanted. I didn't know how the book was going to end. These are all things that are critical to the underlying foundation of a book. I mean, it was almost like I hadn't done my own Nine Box Outline on the book.

Mostly, though, all this creative ennui was because I had fallen out of the habit of engaging with the book and its characters. They weren't haunting my brain like they should be. I was just this guy who showed up and did transcription. But I wasn't committed to the work.

Why? Because I'd gotten into a deep-seated panic about getting things done. Every day, the noise in my head was: *Oh shit! Get stuff done! Get it done now! There isn't time to dally. The clock is ticking. You've only got a couple decades left. Why are you screwing around? You should be writing writing writing! You don't have time to . . .*

I finally put on the brakes and asked an important question. What didn't I have time to do? Actually write the book?

Come on. What sort of nonsense is that?

But that was the loop my brain was on, and it was a bad loop. It was a habit I had made for myself, and it was—clearly—a bunch of noise that was killing my creative drive. I had to break that loop before I had any hope of getting work done.

You have to know where you are in your psychic landscape. You have to know which way you should be pointing, and you have to know the route you should take to reach your goal. But you also have to be honest with yourself about everything else around you—both internally and externally. Honestly, *everything else* is *not* your goal and is *not* part of your path.

It really is that binary: Am I on the path or not?

If you say *no*, then the next step is easy: what do I have to do to get on the path?

If you say *yes*, then rock on.

If you say *no, but* . . . or *yes, but* . . . stop right there. A but statement is dissembling. It's waffling. It's trying to squirm out of one thing by pretending it is another. That doesn't work.

Look at your writing chair. Your butt is either in it or not. You don't perch on the arm of the chair when you say *yes, but* . . ., do you? I suppose you could, but why?

Why do you let yourself squirm away from answering this question honestly?

Are you on the path or not?

So, take a deep breath, and let's do the answer again.

If you want to add the 'but,' go ahead. But—haha! if you get to use it, so do I— listen to yourself as you rattle off whatever ridiculous excuse you're going to be try to sell here. It's a good excuse, and it might even qualify as "creative writing," but it's still an excuse. And you're still not being firm with yourself.

Now, I'm being somewhat facetious when I call it a "ridiculous excuse." There are many reasons why this "but" is creeping into your answer, and some of them have legitimate weight and may not be things you can blithely sweep aside, but—aha! again!—does this "but" precede an excuse or an actual obstacle.

If your words sound like *but it's hard* or *but I don't know what I'm doing* or *but it might suck*, then let's acknowledge those words for what they are: they are merely an expression of the unknown. Which is totally okay. The unknown is pretty much everything more than fifteen seconds in the future, and it's totally weird and different and not what any of us planned.

We like plans. That's what all that stuff roaring around our heads is, anyway. Cool writer plans. And the unknown may not look like that. It probably won't. It'll be something different, and—I know, I know—what if it isn't as cool as what you're imagining?

Look, letting go of this fear is really hard. Yes, what we imagine may not make it on to the page. Yes, you don't know what you're doing. And yes, it might not work *at all* when it actually lands on the page, but . . .

Who cares?

The "but" is fear talking. You give it life with your "but." You feed and nourish it with your "but."

You can also take away its power with your "but."

I'm afraid to write because it might suck, but it will probably be better.

Yes, it is hard but I'm a goddamned Amazon and Amazons eat this shit for breakfast.

Yes, I don't know what I'm doing, but neither does any other writer out there (including the guy writing this book, by the way).

You're a writer, for crying out loud. Making up shit is what you do.

Stop making up negative shit. Make, uh, positive shit.

Whatever. Don't let the swearing distract you from the message. Just as you make up reasons to *not* write, you can make up reasons *to* write. You can find that fire within you. You know it is there. You found it once before. Sure, you're all old and wrinkly now—filled with so much Yoda wisdom that you can't be bothered with getting the words out in their proper order—but that doesn't mean the fire has gone out. The fire never goes out. You're just old and wrinkly and have forgotten where you put it.

Go find it. Find your way. Be honest with yourself about why a book is working or not.

And then—for the love of God—fix it.

Do the work. If you've done it before, then go find your notes. If you haven't done it before, break it down into steps that you do know how to do. If you still don't know what you are doing, admit it and go get help. Read a book (this one, perhaps). Ask your peers. Deconstruct a book or a story by a writer you love, and figure out how they did what they did. It's not all about blasting words onto the page. It's about making story work, and story is a mad squirrel that runs from tree to tree like it is high on meth and nut dust.

You have to trust yourself. You have to know where you want to go. You have to admit when you're lost, and you have to take a deep breath and find your way again.

You got this.

PERMISSION

They say you need to write a million words of crap before you can produce a book worth reading. They say you should only write what you know. They say most of us will never earn out—which is to say, we'll never sell enough copies to warrant the time and effort we spend on these projects. They say . . .

They say a lot of things, but who is "they"?

Well, let's yank back the curtain and take a look.

First, we have Lack-of-Confidence, a sniveler of the finest order. This one's always yanking your earlobe and whispering in your ear. Talking crap all the time. Making you second guess yourself. And yet, Lack-of-Confidence can't even tie their own shoes, for crying out loud.

Next, we have an unholy trinity: This-Sucks, You-Don't-Know-What-You-Are-Doing, and Quick!-Hide-Before-Someone-Realizes-You-Don't-Deserve-To-Be-Here. They finish each other's sentences—and it's cute for ten minutes or so—but they are a walking death trap. Don't get sucked into their conversation. You'll never be heard from again. Ever.

Lurking behind them is Self-Doubt, the ringleader of this awful gang. Self-Doubt has a fancy shirt and new sneakers, but that shirt is way out of style and that much hair product is someone compensating for something, you know?

Anyway, these are the yahoos who are making all the pronouncements about what you can and can't do as a writer. If you like hanging out with these turkeys, by all means, listen to them. But honestly? They only want to be your friend because you're cooler than they are. They're so full of spite and fear and desperation that they're going to drag you do the moment they can get their hands on you.

That's right: they aren't friends; they're concrete shoes. Or albatrosses, depending on which metaphor works better for you.

Which is to say, the only person you need permission from to be a writer is YOU. Every time you have a reason for not being a writer—or not writing, or not doing research, or not learning how to market your books—is because YOU'VE absorbed some comment about how you can't do what you want to do. You've swallowed some vile bit of negativity, let it swirl around in your stomach for awhile, and have now barfed it back up as a platitude of your own making.

And that's just wrong.

Why? Well, first of all, you've just barfed up a platitude. That's gross.

Second of all, this platitude—all slickered up with stomach slime—is not worth hosing off and trying to polish. It will never shine. It will never be something you want to share with someone else. And if you do? They're going to notice you didn't get all the barf cleaned off.

Third—seriously? You need a third reason? Okay. If you hadn't barfed up this platitude, it would have worked its way through eighteen miles of intestines, until it eventually came out your . . . your—well, never mind that.

Our point, circuitously, is this: if you want to write, you can write. You should write.

You are the creative spark that will burn forever, creating such a plume smoky words that your word-making can be seen from space!

And this is all well and good, we know, but—are you tired of the "buts" yet?—but how does freeing yourself from the damning claws of these perpetually obtuse idiots actually help you write?

Well, it's the first step, and you've gotta take that first one if you are going to take a second. In fact, we're going to take four steps.

STEP ONE

The first step in giving yourself permission to be a writer is to stand in front of a mirror and say, "I give myself permission to make shit up."[4]

---

[4] I've tried to write this line without swearing, and frankly, I can't do it without feeling like I'm trying to make a cat vomit. There is going to be some swearing, because that's how I do it. Sorry. Also, this is one of the few places where if the process works for me, I'm going to suggest it might work for you, too. *Caveat elixir*, and all that.

Say this out loud. Make it a mantra. Say in front of some friends. Say it to some fellow writers. When you say something out loud, it sounds different than it does in your head. It sounds *more real.*

Here's the thing about talking to yourself: you tend to leave stuff out. You skip over the awkward bits, and you forget to articulate the true core of what is really nagging you. When you say the words out loud, you have to form complete sentences, which leads to complete thoughts. You can't skim. You have to articulate what it is that you are trying to say.

Here's the thing about making shit up. It's equivalent to saying that you don't know what you are doing. That you aren't an expert. That you don't know how you're going to resolve that plot point in the third act. In fact, it's currently inconceivable how this book is going to get finished in less than a hundred million words, and *oh god!* the submission guidelines say it has to be less than 85K!

The core truth behind "I'm going to make shit up" is that you are going to make something happen. You are going to create something that did not exist. And you know what? No one ever gets it right the first time.

Nor the second, third, fourth, or eighty-fifth. They might get close—which is a result of what? that's right: practice—but it's not going to be perfect. It will *be*, and that's something new. Something that is different. This new state of *being* is much more solid than "you know, I have this idea and it's awesome, but I don't know how to structure a novel of political intrigue in a kingdom inhabited by intelligent starfish and polychromatic squids, and so I'm going to flail around a bit like a squid and then curl up into a ball and wait for everyone to leave."

Here's a secret: no one knows how to structure a book like that. There's no harm in being the first to figure it out.

STEP TWO

After you have given yourself permission to be creative, you must take a deep breath and say, "Now I am going to carve out some time to make shit up." Because creativity doesn't happen in an instant. It's a torturous process in which we must spin vast spindles of word thread; we must darn the thousand socks of the phraseopedes—the multi-legged, articulate insectoids that do the physical work of arranging all the word thread in sequential order; and we must soften the pulp of the blackleaf until it can be chewed into a paste that will form the page upon which the phraseopedes will perform their soft-shoed dance.

Or something like that.

Anyway, we're talking about time. Making shit up takes time, and time is the only precious resource that you have some control over. Whether you keep or give away your time is YOUR decision, and the management of this rare commodity is critical for creatives.

When you announce this second step out loud, you must do it in front of those who have the ability to influence your time. "Hello my darling children, today, your esteemed parent is going to give you Jell-O cups and a couple of Disney DVDs because you must leave me the [REDACTED] alone for thirty minutes so I can have my creative time."

Remember, it's not bad parenting if they have a) food, and b) something shiny to distract them from dismantling the world. This holds true for larger "children," who should be able to manage themselves for a few hours after a couple dozen years of wandering about this planet, for crying out loud.

You must articulate what you need in order to be creative. Is it a half hour chunk of time in the evening? Is it a room where you can go and close the door for an hour and not be disturbed? Is it a matter of telling social media to stop sucking your soul for an afternoon? No matter the external influences and claim-layers to your time, they must be told that you are taking some time for yourself.

Sure, it make look like a negotiation, but that's all for show. You've already given yourself permission to make shit up, and you've already told yourself that you are going to use YOUR OWN DAMN TIME to do so. You are, in fact, merely informing the rest of the world of your intentions. If it makes them feel better to be a "concerned party who has been informed and heard" in this matter, whatever. It's the emotional version of giving them a pat on the head and a Jell-O cup.

You've done your duty.

STEP THREE

Once you have gone to that magical place where shit gets made, you will have to return. I know. You can't stay in make-believe land forever. You have to come back, and you have to assess what this thing is that you made while you were there. And yes, maybe it is, literally, shit. That's okay. It merely means you are ready to take the third step.

This is the moment where you give yourself permission to be human—to be fallible, inconsistent, frightened, and prone to dreaming far grander than your current skills can manage. Take a deep breath and admit this to yourself.

Then, look at this . . . this steaming pile of word goo.

Be honest. It's going to need some work.

Look, I know the fabulous stuff you have in your head is totally perfect. Socrates rambled on about this, back in his day. He yammered on about the Cave and how light from torches cast shadows. These shadows are only imperfect representations of the Ideal, which is something we can't see, but which we Know is there. All things have a perfect form, and the more abstract they are—the less *formed* they are—the closer they are to perfection.

But when that story—filled with all those fabulous ideas—flops out of your head and lies there on the page? Yeah, not so perfect.

But that's okay, because you have to make something before you can fix.

Writers write, and thinkers think. There's a big difference between "I think I have a good idea," and "Well, that third act is a mess, and the world-building is powered by a bunch of giant hamsters whacked out on amphetamines."

The latter example is something that can be fixed. The former is just an idea, and ideas are just star stuff, really.

STEP FOUR

And now, the final step. Free yourself! Shed those shackles! It is time to give yourself permission to ignore what others think of the shit you made up.

Sure, the world-building is totally powered by giant drug-addled hamsters, but world-building is hard. It's not like eating tacos or trash talking the last two minutes of a closely contested Super Bowl.

No one gets to talk badly of something you created, because you did it and they didn't. That's it. Any of those voices who speak ill of you are just like those five idiots you jettisoned a long time ago. Sure, occasionally, someone with a credible amount of critical thinking skills may point out some aspect of your book that didn't quite work, but that's merely an observation about craft that you can employ on the next thing you do.

Because, as we noted early, no one makes the perfect story. Everyone makes the best story they can, at the time they made it. "Sure, I didn't bother closing the narrative arc of the main secondary character, but whatever, I'll get it on the next book."

Newton's First Law says that an object in motion tends to stay in motion, and an object at rest tends to stay at rest.

Be the first part of that law and not the second. Make shit up. Keep making shit up.

You have my permission.

Not that you need it.

PRODUCTIVITY

Okay, so now that we've given ourselves permission to go write, we can do that, yes? We've got notes! We've got an outline! If we did the *Jumpstart Your Novel* Nine Box Outline, we've got lots and lots of notes. This book has practically written itself, hasn't it?[5]

Well, not exactly.

We know what the book looks like. We know its structure, and we have a reasonable sense of what has to happen in what order. But the actual parade of words across the page—all eighty or ninety or a hundred thousand of them—still has to be done. And if you're like me, you have no idea where you're going to find the time to actually do all this work. In fact, having built this chart probably drives home the point that you really don't know when or how you're going to finish this book. Which is completely understandable. What you've got on the page in front of you is a LOT of work, and some of it is probably

---

[5] Not to plug the previous book again, but *ahem* you should—well, let's not belabor the point. But you can check out APPENDIX B for a chart that wll help you create a sprawling note-filled document.

still completely vague and filled with magical hand-waving with a liberal application of mystical "shit."

"OMG, it's not a book!" you wail. "Damn you, Teppo! You lied to me. It's just more notes!"

Hold on, there, Skippy. Actually, what've you've got there is a roadmap. Think of it as a process chart that tells you exactly what happens, and in what order. The trick is figuring out how to turn this roadmap into actual words. To accomplish that, we need to get our butts in our chairs and get some writing done. Since we've told ourselves that we have the skills and we've given ourselves permission, that means we should talk about time management.

Oh, managing time. First, we invent the whole concept of time, and then we turn around and create an entire industry devoted to teaching you how to better manage this artificial construct we invented in the first place. Weren't our lives easier before we got all this high-tech awareness of the eternal half-life decay of the cesium atom? Back when we were all preternaturally young and beautiful and lived stress free lives down by the water.

But, alas, we can't undo this awareness, and so we have become both the keepers of time and the wasters of time. What we have to do is learn to focus on the former and stop celebrating being the latter.

I could spend a couple of hours harranguing you about time management and list management and all those other aspects of personal management that will make you a highly productive, whirlwind self-manager, but that's not why we're here. We're here to talk about writing, and so we'll only dally for a mere moment on the topic of time management. We'll keep it simple, which means a modicum of math and some earnest aphorisms.

Time, for all of its metaphysical and philosophical ephemerality, has a very real presence in our lives. We treat it as if it were a quantifiable object. "I don't have time for this," we say. "How much time is this meeting going to take?" "When was the last time you bathed?" We have watches and clocks and floating displays on our computer screens constantly reminding us of the passage of time. And we always moan about not having enough.

Enough of what? If we substituted "jelly beans" for "time" in the previous sentences, you'd think I was spouting nonsense. "I don't have the jelly beans for this." What does that even mean?

Well, it means I need more jelly beans, right? And if I could go to the store and buy more beans, then I'd be able to surmount the "this"—this obstacle I'm facing. Sounds easy.

But when I put "time" in for "jelly beans," then going to store isn't a solution. You can't buy more time. You can't even manufacture it, which leads to all sorts of other difficult questions.

But let's not go there. Let's back up and ask a simple question: why can't I buy more time?

★

Let's shift gears for a minute and talk about to-do lists. These lists range from grocery lists to complex Gantt project management charts. The fundamental unit of each and every list is the line item. A grocery list—"bread," "milk," eggs," "spatula," "cat food"—is a list of items that can be bought at a grocery store. This list might be a subset of another list, the "Things To Do Before I Go Home" list. By going to the grocery store and getting each of those five items, I get to check off "go to grocery store" from my other list, but I don't get to check that item off until I've checked off all the items on the grocery sub-list.

Put another way: I can only do one list at a time. More importantly, regardless of how things are nested, I am only doing one list item on any given list at any given time.

Now, someone will pipe up from the back about multi-tasking and efficiency models and all that, and yes, that's what all the time management books prattle on about. Regardless of what those earnest tomes tell you about multitasking and split brain efficiency though, you are still only doing *one* thing at any given moment.

If our lives were Gantt charts, "Go To The Grocery Store" would be a line item with multiple dependencies. These dependencies would form a sub-list—"get bread," "get milk," "get eggs," "get spatula for secret nighttime project," "get food for that small mammal that makes funny noises at night." We're being efficient when we group these items under "Go To The Grocery Store," but while we were walking up and down the aisle at the store, searching for bread, we were not also searching for spatulas.

Maybe we'll pass the spatulas, and think: "Oh hey, spatulas! They're on my list." And we'll re-order our processes to chose a spatula, check it off our list, and continue our search for bread.

A to-do list is a simple structure. Each item is listed on a single line. *I'm going to do X, and then I'm going to do Y, and after that, I'll do Z.* Sure, multitasking may let you do X and Y and Z all at once, but let's be kind to ourselves here. If X and Y and Z are chapters in the book, you can only write one of them at a time, right?

It boils down this: You have to focus on the task in front of you, and there can only be one task.

You could look at your list of chapters and treat them like looking for bread and finding spatulas in the store, but chapters in a book aren't quite the same as random household goods on grocery store shelves. Unlike bread and spatulas, chapters have an internal dependency built in. The reader has to move through them in sequential order because that is how the narrative works. I know people who write their chapters out of order—they hop from scene to scene [6]—and there's certainly nothing wrong with writing a book this way IF IT WORKS FOR YOU.

The important thing here is to recognize that each chapter is a distinct item on your list, and in order to complete the list, you have to check off each chapter as an individual unit.

---

[6] Which is craziness, of course. But it doesn't negate the point I'm making here, so don't get confused by those fruitbats who write shit completely nonsensically.

I'm being pedantic here to make a point, so bear with me for a little bit. A chapter is a line item on your list of to-dos. It is a collection of words that is a required unit of the overall book.

I like to work with eighteen chapters, and I arbitrarily assign 5,000 words to each chapter so that I end up with a 90,000 word book. I end up with more or less "chapters" because some scenes run long and some run short. I don't worry about that overmuch because the number of chapters isn't important. Nor is the word count per chapter. What is important is that "chapter X" is a line item on the list that is "Write the Book."

A chapter is merely a unit that we can do some math with. Like this:

total word count / chapters = words per chapter

Once we have the number of words that make up a chapter, let's figure out how long it takes us to make those words. Normally, I tend to write about 1,000 words an hour, and this is a "rough draft, banging on the keyboard and making the words appear" sort of pace. Okay, so how fast I write (rate) times the number of words in the book (length) equals number of hours required to write the book.

Or:

length / rate = total hours to finish a draft

Doing some math now, I can see that it'll take me ninety hours to write this book. That seems like a lot, I know, but let's break it down.

How about one hour a day? If I write an hour a day, five days a week, it'll take me eighteen weeks to write this book. That's four and a half months.

Now, if I did that week in and week out, I'd finish three books a year. What? That's kind of cool, in't it? Three books a year! Wow.

But what if I wrote on the weekends too? At seven hours a week—let's see, carry the four, add a zero here—I'm going to finish the book in less than thirteen weeks. What? I've just saved a month of time!

Since it only takes me three months to write the book, that means *I could write an extra book a year.*

I'm just mathing. I'm not making stuff up. I'm not even inventing time that doesn't exist. It's all right there—right in those 8,760 hours that are in every year.

Even if you stare at the ceiling for a third of those hours (2,920 of them) and work at a full-time job for another third (another 2,920, plus commuting time and lunch breaks), there are still 2,920 hours of every year that are unaccounted for.

I'm not trying to make you feel bad about your time management skills or pass judgment on how busy your life is. I'm just noting the amount of butt in chair time needed to write a book is about 3.2% of the available hours in a given year. It's not even 5%.

Why is that 5% so hard to find?

Well, there's a couple hundred thousand reasons, and many of them are completely valid, but a lot of them also fall into the broad category of Spurious Time Suckage. Let's sidestep talking about STS for a moment and focus on something much better: Glorious Writing Time.

EXERCISE

Do the math for your book. How fast do you write? How long is your book? How many hours will it take for you finish a draft?

Look at your schedule for any given day. How many hours do you sleep? How many hours do you work? How much commuting time is there? How long does it take you to cram a piece of toast in your mouth in the morning while you try to find a clean outfit? How long does it take to reheat dubious looking leftovers from last week? Do you go to the gym, and if so, for how long?

Once all those hours have been accounted for, how many hours are left?

Multiply that number by .05. This is the 5% rule.

Given your current schedule, this is the amount of time (in fractions of an hour) that you can—and you don't need any justification to do so—give yourself for writing. If you have four hours a day that aren't otherwise allocated, then 5% of those four hours is twelve minutes.

This is the baseline definition of Glorious Writing Time, and you should give yourself a minimum of one unit of GWT a day.

At a rate of one thousand words an hour, these twelve minutes mean you are going to write 200 words. If you are writing a 90,000 word book, then it will take you approximately one year and three months to write your book.

That's what the math says. That's your goal.

If you are like me, however, that goal isn't good enough. That's the minimum, right? Surely we can do better than that. Doing better, however, requires more butt in chair time, which means improving our GWT value.

SPACE

But before we do that, let's take a moment and talk about space. There is lots of room to rattle around in space and get nothing done. Why? Because Space is big and dark. In some ways, it would be nice to get rid of all that extra space, because then you would haven't worry about it being big and dark.

We've already covered giving yourself permission, and we've done some math to figure out how much time it is going to take us to write, but there's one last thing to consider: where you write.

It's important to have space to think. There are lots of reasons for this, some of which are obvious, right? If your brain is filled up with all manner of lists and worries and apprehensions, it is going to be difficult to think about writing a book.[7] It's going to be even harder to think about finishing a book. And so, we've got to find some precious space where we can do some thinking.

---

[7] Naturally, none of what you've read here is adding to your worries and apprehensions, of course. And the lists we've made? Totally manageable, right?

At first, beyond giving yourself permission to write, you need to learn how to clear your mind of everything else so that you can write. It's one thing to tell yourself to go off and make word magic, it's another thing to get your brain to come along for the fun. But the brain has to come too, otherwise, you're going to spend an hour staring out the window, wondering how catastrophic a mess all your to-dos are making on the living room carpet. So how do we achieve this impossible nirvana?

Well, we can do some breathing exercises. We can meditate. We can play hopscotch. Or drink scotch.[8] There are many ways to get your brain primed for making words, and I heartily recommend you try a few things out. Find something that works well for you.

Write that amazing secret down, for crying out loud. You're going to forget, or you're going to be stressed, and it will be hard to get into the proper writing head space. A written cue will help calm your brain. *You did it once; you can do it again* is the conversation you want to with your brain, and that slip of paper is going to hold up the first part of your argument. Your brain can *la-la-la* all it likes, but it's hard to ignore words on a page, because they're real.

SIXTY SECONDS DOING DEEP BREATHING EXERCISES WHILE SEATED IN A PARTIAL LOTUS POSE GETS ME IN THE MOOD.

---

[8] Well, maybe not that last one. Save that for after you've done the day's work.

Partial Lotus because, you know, stiff knees.

Once you've written this secret of the universe down, practice it. Go off and do the thing it says, and then after doing that, write.

Ah, but where are you going to write? Well, that's a very good question, because where you write is equally as important as how and when you write.

Just as your brain will distract you from making happy words, so, too, will your surroundings. We know a writer who once wrote on the train, and when they stopped riding the train, they stopped writing. It baffled this writer, and he raged about town like a dyslexic dinosaur trying to spell "MISSISSIPPI," and no one was happy. It wasn't until he remembered that he knew how to write on the train that he started to think about how that worked.

It took him a little while, because, you know, *dinosaur*, but eventually, he remembered what the physical environment was like on the train. He sat at a table, where he was surrounded by other people, who insisted on talking very loudly about things like local sports teams and other people who had pissed them off at their jobs, and how terrible the weather was. The writer didn't care about any of that, and in fact, he drowned it all out by listening to bands like Tarmvred, Winterkälte, and Converter.[9]

---

[9] But not Merzbow, because at soft volumes, it's like listening to someone scratch ten penny nails on a chalkboard. At high volumes, it's like all the grooves on your brain are being scraped off. Good for some, I suppose, but not for this writer. One must know one's limits when it comes to Rhythmic Noise and Power Electronics.

Basically, he put himself in a box that he couldn't escape and tuned out everything else so that there was nothing else to do but write.

After a little trial and error, he discovered that the comfy chair by the fireplace in Starbucks between the hours of nine in the morning and noon were a rough equivalent of being sardined in the train on the morning commute. And his productivity went way up.

Think about the places where you have been productive. What is it about them that makes them work for you? What is it about other places that makes them less productive? We find it hard to write at home, because it is easy to be distracted by things that need cleaning or washing or vacuuming.

Figure out where you are most comfortable in your writing skin and go there. Make that space. Fill it with your magic writing being.

And if there are other people who inhabit that space, well, you might have to negotiate with them to ensure that you have writing time. Which goes back to permission models and closed doors and signs that say, "Writing Time Is On. Make Your Own Damn Breakfast."

Tame that physical space. Just as you have tamed your brain. Body and mind, grasshopper. And then all the word making can happen.

GLORIOUS WRITING TIME

The singular secret to finishing your book is putting your butt in a chair and writing. It doesn't matter if you use a laptop, a desktop machine, a tablet, or an Etch-a-Sketch. It doesn't matter if you write longhand with a pencil, pen, crayon, or silver-tipped stylus dipped in blood. All that matters is that you have a method for getting words get out of your brain and onto the page.

Nothing else matters. That's the simplest rule of the universe. You write, therefore, the book gets finished.

Previously, we established a unit that we called Glorious Writing Time—the GWT. The time it takes to write a book is measured by a number of GWTs, and what differs from writer to writer (and book to book, for that matter), is the real world span of time that is each unit of GWT.

If your GWT is only twelve minutes, then it's going to take you a little while to write 100,000 words. If your GWT is four hours, then we all expect you to have that book finished by Thursday. It's all relative, and there is no correct answer other than knowing the length of time that is one unit of GWT.

This is your basic bargaining chip with the universe.

In fact, I would recommend buying a set of poker chips. Whatever color they have the most of is your single unit of GWT. Let's say these are the red chips. Blue chips are worth five red ones. Green are worth five blue. Black are worth five green. And so on.

These chips making the negotiating real. Your support structure will understand these tokens more readily than some nebulous argument that you have to "go write."[10]

Not too long ago, my kids reached that age where they weren't going to tolerate an all-day day care program. They were going to be around all damn day, which meant an endless parade of feet up and down the stairs. Oh, and the questions. Dear God, the questions.

"Dad: can we have ice cream?"

"Dad: can X come over?"

"Can I go over to X's house?"

"Can X and I go back and forth between our house and their house every half hour?"

"Dad: can we rent a pony for the summer."

Non-stop.

Guess who wasn't getting any work done?

I had to figure out how to get work done with all that going around me. I made up a bunch of prize cards, showed them to the kids, and then put them in a box.

---

[10] To them, "writing" is you staring at a computer screen for an hour and bitching at them for interrupting you, when all they see you doing is trying to hide the fact that you're playing some Facebook game. This gets a little hard to justify.

"Now for every blue chip you earn, you get to draw a card from the box," I told them.

"How do we get blue chips?" they asked.

"You earn five red chips," I said.

"And how do we get red ones?" they asked.

"For every half hour of uninterrupted time that I get, you earn a red chip," I said. "If you solve a conflict between yourselves over who poked who first without yelling 'Dad!,' you get a red chip. If you can manage to not slam the front door during the endless to and fro-ing, you get a chip. Got it?"

They got it, and at the end of the day, they had both earned enough chips for a blue one, and they drew cards that said "Fro-Yo!" I was the best dad EVER! Total cost for childcare that day? $10.00.

All day daycare would have been $80.00 to $100.00.

By the third day, my daughter was harassing me for not working enough so they could earn chips. Bonus!

They certainly didn't keep track of my time; they just wanted to know that chips were going into the box. How did I count the chips? I gave myself two reds for every unit of GWT, which was 1,000 words or about an hour of work time.

The important thing about GWT is that it doesn't have to be "writing" time. It can be editing time. It can be email time. It can be web design time. It can be social media marketing time. It is a unit of time that you spend on your career. Most of them should be devoted to writing, but a unit is a unit, and you can spend it anyway you like.

But it is VITALLY IMPORTANT that you assign an activity to that unit of GWT. If you tell yourself that you're going to spend an hour on the computer doing "important things," and not identify explicitly what those things are, do you know what is going to happen? You're going to spend the hour getting lost in a Wikipedia rabbit hole and get nothing done.

Get a timer. Assign a task to the GWT. ONLY DO THAT TASK for the duration of the GWT.

I'm going to say this again: *you can only do one thing at a time when you are working on a to-do list.* A unit of GWT can only be used to clear ONE line item from your list. Your time is valuable, and if you don't keep a close watch on it, then it will get away from you.

It is very easy, in our busy lives, to let non-essential goals slip, and for us, these are the writer goals. If we don't have the time to get the critical stuff done, how are we going to have time to write? The more we try to figure out the answer to this question, the more the answer slips away. This adds stress, which is exactly what we need more of, right? And more stress leads to more overthinking and huffing into a paper bag and wringing our hands and cat vacuuming and ... and ... and!

Remember when I said you should look at the world in a very simple way? Your butt is in the chair, or it isn't. Nothing else matters. This is the simplicity of the GWT, because, why? It is Glorious Writing Time.

I have a little sheet with nine empty boxes on it. In the morning, I write an activity in each of these boxes. "Email,"

"Website content," "House work," "Errands"—whatever it is that I'd like to accomplish that day. In the rest of the boxes, I write "Make the Words!" This is my GWT chart for the day.

Maybe these are hour-long boxes. Maybe they are half hour boxes. It doesn't matter. When I am in one of those boxes, that's the only thing I am working on. I can't leave the box until the task is done, and when it is, I get to cross that box off. At any point in the day, I can look at my sheet and see exactly how productive I've been.[11]

Many of my projects can't be completed in one unit of GWT. I don't scrawl "write book" in one box, and then get furious when it's not done in an hour. I check my magic chart to see where I'm at in the book, and then I write "half of Chapter Six," or "that stupid scene that is dogging me in Chapter 11." For any other project that I'm working on, I break that project down into line items that can reasonably fit in one unit of GWT.

- Copy edit 10 pages of a manuscript.
- Research comparisons for an upcoming title.
- Fill out the fields in the distributor's intake system.
- Build the front/back matter bookmap for a title.
- Write half a chapter.
- Make chili for dinner.
- Do two loads of laundry.
- Read a book, because reading is important, too.

---

[11] See APPENDIX B for the Nine Box Model chart.

I try to assign writing time to at least half the boxes, and when I'm ready to start the day's boxes, I do one or two writing boxes first. Then I take a break, and do one or two of the other boxes. Then, another box of writing, and then a few other boxes. If I clear them all quickly, then I get that last box of writing in—and I leave that one open-ended. I can write and write and write and write. Why? Because I've filled in eight other boxes—I've earned the equivalent of eight red poker chips.

I bought a lot of frozen yogurt that summer, but that was all right by me. I got a lot of words written too.

EXERCISE

Get a blank sheet of paper. Tear it half so that you have two pieces that are 8.5" tall by 5.5" wide. Draw three rows of three boxes on each sheet. You will notice there is not a lot of space on the page for anything else. This is on purpose. Label one sheet "Tomorrow" and the other one "The Day After." Fill out the nine boxes on each with nine things that you would like to accomplish in your GWT sessions over the next two days.

Check off the boxes as necessary.

Give yourself a reasonable self-assessment at the end of the second day on how you did. Adjust your definition of a unit of GWT, if necessary.

Repeat until the book is complete. Easy peasy lemon squeezy.

PART TWO

TALKING ABOUT STRUCTURE

PLANTING SEEDS

PART ONE OF THIS BOOK WAS ABOUT THE ROOT STRUCTURE of your book. Even though we didn't talk about actual book stuff, we talked about how your book is going to be supported. If these words are going to grow, then they need a good environment and a daily dose of sunlight and fresh air.

Now, we're going to talk about what grows from that fecund soil you've planted and carefully fertilized. Novels are like topiaries, small trees that have been sculpted from natural materials into specific shapes as imagined by their creators.[12]

However, if a novel is allowed to grow out of control, the branches get tangled. The bark gets all gnarled, and whatever fruit this tree is growing turns out to be sour and nasty. Before you know it, there's a squirrel living in the trunk, and those damn neighborhood kids are carving their initials in the bark.

That's not going to be your tree.

---

[12] But more like balloon animals than the twisted topiaries from the Overlook Hotel, right?

You want a tree that grows within well-established boundaries. You want something that grows tall and proud, with a heavy canopy of broad leaves that provide shade year round. You want people to gather beneath your tree and marvel at its thick trunk and hearty branches.

All of which is to say: that book you slammed out while pinging GWT chips into the hat? It needs a little attention. It needs some shaping and pruning. We need to make sure it doesn't send out little tendrils that turn into other books. It needs to draw sustenance from the roots you have grown within the soil.

Imagine the writer as a tree farmer. Not the sort who manages a whole orchard or an entire forest. But a specialist. You've got one tree, and you're in charge of it from the moment it first gets planted.

It starts out from a tiny nut, a single point from which the rest of the structure will grow. This is our foundation, our world-building nut. Is it healthy? Is it fully formed?

Now, you don't have to know every minute detail of your world, but know enough to make informed decisions about your characters and how they react to stimuli within the world. It is easy to get lost in world-building, after all, and you need some of it to ground yourself. But remember that you should be writing. Dreaming up backstory and world-building can easily become a distraction.

To be safe, let's keep it brief. It's a nut you planted, remember? Nuts aren't that big.

What is this book? Maybe it is "steampunk with giant bears," or "the Wild West with zombies," or "it's New

York City in the 1950s, but in a world where WWII never happened." Whatever. Write it down on a notecard and file it somewhere. You never have to tell anyone, but it's there, all the same.[13]

While we're talking about grounding ourselves, let's take a moment and put ourselves in the reader's shoes. When a reader picks up a book, they are engaging in a conversation with a writer—one that may grow into a long-term relationship, or one that may only last a few hours. While the writer starts the conversation, the reader finishes it, and the conversation the writer thought they are starting might not be the conversation the reader wants to have. Additionally, readers may discover the conversation they thought they were having with the writer might not be what y'all are going to end up talking about. Some readers don't like this; others delight in discovering this twist.

Regardless, a writer has to establish some ground rules for the conversation in the beginning of the book. They have to provide the scope, nature, and duration of the conversation, because readers want to know what they are getting into. It's a very natural series of questions that

---

[13] "But what about research?" you cry. Look, I like research. I like it a lot, and I used to do a lot of research before I started. Well, I bought a lot of books that I intended to read for research, but I rarely got around to most of them. Partly because I'm lazy, but also because as I wrote the book, I discovered that it was going in a different direction or that it wasn't going deep enough into the topic that I needed to read all six thousand pages that I had on the shelf. Nowadays, I try to wait until I'm fairly confident in the direction of the narrative or the shape of a scene before I disappear into the research hole.

Research is an excuse for not writing. Recognize it for what it is, and treat it accordingly. I know. I am the Fun-Wrecker.

a reader is going to have, and the writer must provide answers for these questions as soon as possible. Otherwise, you risk losing the reader.

One of the simplest ways of answering these questions is through setting. When a reader opens a book, they are going to have three questions which the writer needs to answer as quickly as possible. These questions are:

- *Where is this book taking place?*
- *When is this book taking place?*
- *What is the relationship between our viewpoint character and this place and time?*

Let's look at some examples:

J. R. R. Tolkien (from that perennial classic, *The Hobbit*)

In a hole in the ground there lived a hobbit. Not a nasty, dirty, wet hole, filled with the ends of worms and an oozy smell, nor yet a dry, sandy hole with nothing in it to sit down on or to eat: it was a hobbit hole, and that meant comfort.

David Baldacci (from 2001's *Last Man Standing*)

Web London held a semiautomatic SR75 rifle custom built for him by a legendary gunsmith. The SR didn't stop at merely wounding flesh and bone;

it distinegrated them. Web would never leave home without this high chieftain of muscle guns, for he was a man steeped in violence. He was always prepared to kill, to do so efficiently and without error. Lord, if he ever took a life by mistake he might as well have eaten the bullet himself, for all the misery it would cause him. Web just had that complex way of earning his daily bread. He couldn't say he loved his job, but he did excel at it.

Jane Austen (from *Pride and Prejudice*)

It is a truth universally acknowledged, that a single man in possession of a good fortune, must be in want of a wife.

However little known the feelings or views of such a man may be on his first entering a neighborhood, this truth is so well fixed in the minds of the surrounding families, that he is considered as the rightful property of some one or another of their daughters.

Robert B. Parker (from 2006's *Hundred-Dollar Baby*)

The woman who came into my office on a bright January day was a knockout. Her hair had blond highlights and her fawn-colored suit appeared to have been hand-sewn by Michael Kors. She took off some sort of fur-lined cape and tossed it over the arm of my couch, and came over and sat down in one of my client chairs. She smiled at me. I smiled at her. She waited. The light coming in my window was especially bright this morning, enhanced by the light snowfall that had collected overnight. She didn't seem dangerous. I remained calm.

Elmore Leonard once offered ten rules about writing, and the first one is "Never open a book with weather." Why? Because readers want to engage with characters. They don't want history lessons. They don't want long passages of flowery prose that merely tells them that writer is of the opinion that they can turn a phrase or two. Readers want to be entertained. They want to engage with stories that aren't their own. They want their imagination stimulated.

As a writer, you refuse to give the readers what they want at your own peril.

Some of the writers in the previous examples mentioned the weather. Some did not. Some engaged us with characters; some set the stage for the events that were to follow. And even though many of them did not explicitly discuss the physical world in which the book was taking place, they gave us clues so that we could ground ourselves.

Look over those examples. What can you identify about the conversation the writer is going to have with their readers from those openings?

Even if you don't know anything about J. R. R. Tolkien's classic fantasy novel, you know that a) it's about a fantastic creature, but one that likes a nice cup of tea and cozy socks. Jane Austen's opening sets the stage for a comedy of class confusion and manners. David Baldacci is writing a thriller of some kind because his character clearly lives in that sort of world. And Robert B. Parker's character—all aloof and enigmatic—is self-assured and knows something about dangerous work.

We can learn much with little. As a writer, you don't have to give readers everything when you start.

TOPIARY ACTION

Anyway, back to our world-building nut. Let's start coaxing something out of that nut, shall we? How about a nice solid central trunk? This is the narrative foundation that grows from our exploration of the protagonist.

Who are they? What external factors are going to shape, influence, or otherwise interact with them? Are there internal factors that will come into play? Who are the other characters, and how are they going to interact with the protagonist? What does the protagonist want? And, in order to fulfill that want, what must the protagonist get?

Look at your chart. You can take the list of chapters and start stacking them up, building the trunk of your tree.

You could keep stacking, but then you're not really making a tree. You're raising a fat stick. We don't want fat sticks for our novels. We want lovely trees with thick branches.

Let's give our tree a pair of branches, and because a union is divided when there is a difference within a homogenous body, let's consider these branches to be mirrors of each other. Branches raised in opposition, if you will.

Let's call one branch "Unity" and the other, "Separation."

We still have the central trunk, of course, and let's call that "Balance"—a structure equidistant between the two branches.

As our tree grows taller, these branches will split into other branches, and some of these branches will reach back to the trunk, entwine with it, and perhaps even stretch out a leaf or two to the other branch. We're making pathways among our branches now. This will create a fuller canopy of leaves, allowing the topiary shape of the tree to be more finely pruned.

And so where the branches from each branch touch the central trunk again, let's call that "Harmony." At some point in your novel, possibly just after the first act, we're going to have a moment where events and characters come together, and everything seems all rosy and stable. This won't last, of course, but let's not forgo the moment where we embrace the stability of this central trunk.[14]

The other branches continue to grow as well. "Unity" remains constant, and if we're building off constancy, then let's mark a point a little farther up that trunk as "Extension." Over on the "Separation" branch, matters have gone a little awry, even though the tree is continuing to grow. Let's just mark this point as "Limitation."

---

[14] Chapter-wise, this is somewhere just shy of halfway. Typically, I write "Sex" in the chapter description when I'm doing the quick chapter rundown. Laugh all you like, but you'll see that this is the chapter where funny stuff happens. And, of course, the next chapter is "Things Get Worse," because they typically do after sex at this point in the narrative.

More growth happens. We're closing in on the third act, and offshoots cross back and forth. Near the end of the second act, the protagonist has been through the crucible of transformation, wherein they've assimilated the knowledge they've gained over the course of the narrative (we'll even label a point somewhere there in the middle as such).

And then, as we pass into the third act, we mark two more points on the branches—"Action" and "Creation"—before all the branches and the central trunk converge once more at a point we'll label as "Resolution."

At this point, your tree diagram may look something like the diagram on the following page.[15]

---

[15] No one should be surprised that I turned this into an diagram with historical esoteric connotations. I'm the guy who convinced you all to buy a deck of Tarot Cards to use for novel outlining in *Jumpstart Your Novel*, after all.

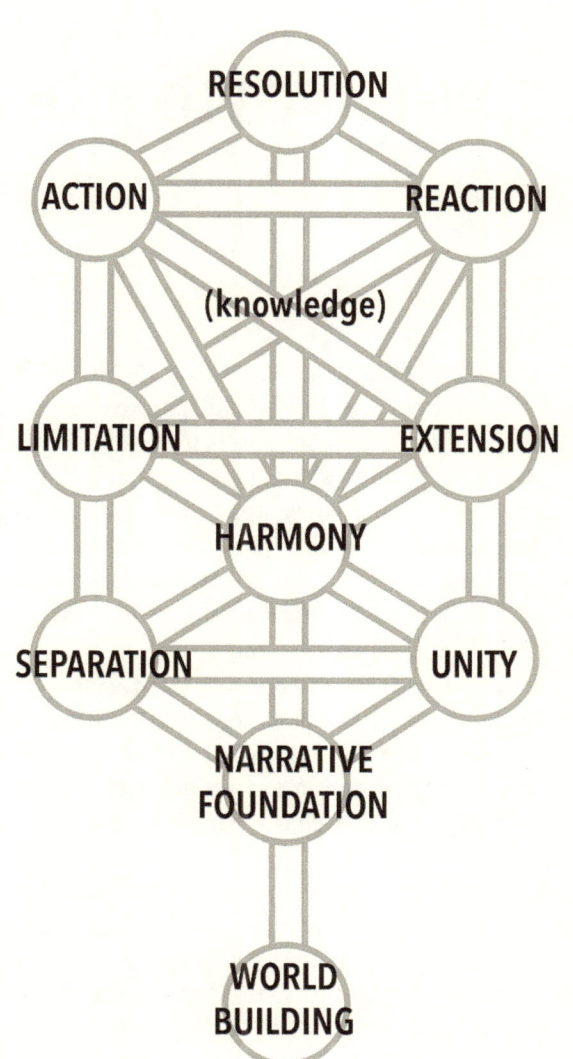

CONNECTING PLOT DOTS

Plotting is merely a sequence of events that happen—one after the other—that connect disparate elements of a narrative arc. Sure, a list of chapters is handy to know the shape of the arc, but the actual procession of events from the beginning to the end may still be very... hazy in your mind. You can fudge it for awhile, but eventually you're going to have to sit down and chart the whole book out. It sounds like work, and it probably is, but you've got a chart, a circle, and now a tree map.

But what is this tree map we just drew? Sure, it looks suspiciously like the Cabalistic Tree of Life, but what does ancient mysticism have to do with writing a book? Well, it's an archetypal foundation to your narrative, for one. It's also a nifty diagram that charts pathways that are part of your narrative.

Look at it this way: each point on this tree leads to other points, and each time you leave a point, you must have another point in mind. And if you pass through a second point on the way to your primary destination, that has an effect within your narrative as well. It's all stuff that has an impact on your story. Yes, it may seem like an arbitrary organizational structure for your story, but—like all narrative structures—it has value and weight because, more often than not, it fits.

Star Wars, for example, starts with Luke Skywalker on Tatooine with some WORLD-BUILDING. And then we get a little NARRATIVE FOUNDATION (the Empire wants stolen plans that are hidden in the brain box of a rogue robot), after which events begin to happen. Luke finds the 'droids, meets Ben Kenobi, and leaves the planet (UNITY).

Alternately, the stormtroopers lose the data and are unable to find the 'droids before they escape the planet (SEPARATION). Meanwhile, Grand Moff Tarkin, feigning lack of concern about the loss of the plans, demonstrates the power of the fully operational battle station on Princess Leia's home planet (EXTENSION). Luke and Ben make new friends (HARMONY), but they are captured by the Death Star before they can get the plans to the rebel alliance (LIMITATION).

All is not lost, as they manage to rescue the princess and escape, but as they are escaping, Vader kills Kenobi,[16] which acts to galvanize the team to finish the mission and deliver the plans to the rebels. The Death Star pursues

---

[16] For the esoteric nerds out there, the spot marked "knowledge" on the tree is known as Da'at, which can be read as either the infinite revelation of the Divine as revealed in the flesh, or the gateway to the Abyss where the seeker is confronted by the possibility of all realities (cf., the Moon in the Tarot).

them (ACTION), and they come up with a working plan to destroy the Death Star (CREATION, also consider this as a REACTION to the ACTION of the other branch), which leads to the final showdown and destruction of the Death Star (RESOLUTION).

Let's not forget that other characters in your novel have narrative arcs as well. Character growth (or, at least, the impression of character growth) isn't limited to your protagonist. Your adversary has an arc too. In fact, I like to think that they are the protagonist of their own narrative arc—it just happens to be in total opposition to the other protagonist's arc.

This is the source of all narrative tension, by the way. Handy, right?

Anyway, the simplest way to blend these two together is to think of the adversary's narrative as always being on the opposite branch from the protagonist at any given point on the tree.[17] You can use the pathways to move back and forth between the points as you progress through your narrative, but each time you stop, the adversary stops too. Each success of the protagonist is a failure for the adversary, and each failure of the protagonist is an opportunity for the adversary to monologue endlessly. As they do.

---

[17] And not only is it critical to consider the adversary as the protagonist of their own arc, but you must treat their arc with the same respect as the protagonist's. Make sure their actions and reactions follow a logical progression of striving to achieve their own goal. Adversaries aren't idiots; they're merely not as clever as the protagonist. Which is to say: their plans would have worked if it hadn't been for those meddling kids . . .

Your narrative structure should move back and forth between both branches of the tree. If it doesn't, you may be writing a fatalistic 19th-century Russian drama about the futility of existence, and while that's probably a crackling good read for when you're in full body traction for a month or two, it's not the sort of book we're working on here. So, set aside your inner Dostoevsky, and let's keep the narrative moving back and forth across the branches of the tree.

Plotting is linear. You go from point to point to point to point. All this talk of trees and branches is to give you tools to use as you move from point to point. Sure, you can write a book that goes from world-building to narrative foundation to resolution, but—hang on, let me just write that one right now.

> *Once upon a time there was a family of goats. They all lived in a beautiful valley filled with tall grasses and leafy trees. They ate the grasses and slept under the trees, living happy, long lives. The end.*

Your book should be longer. Therefore, it is going to need to hit a few more plot points.

Back in the day, there was a man named William Wallace Cook who was an even more prolific pulp writer than Lester Dent. Unlike Dent, who devised the fairly straightforward Master Plot Outline, Cook devised a dizzyingly complex master plot matrix he called *Plotto*. It starts with a fairly basic theory—"Purpose, opposed by Obstacle, yields Conflict"—but once you get into the minutiae of the opposition part, Plotto turns into a rabbit hole of available paths from A to B to C (almost 1,500, in fact). Cook wrote 40,000 word dime novels that were all sixteen chapters long (and each chapter was exactly five pages of single-spaced type). This is the model of a man who has a plan. You can have one too.[18]

EXERCISE

Map your narrative arc to the tree diagram. Start at a high level and assign a critical chapter to enough of the points that you can follow a path up the tree. Imagine that everything between NARRATIVE FOUNDATION and the pair of ACTION and REATION is your second act.

Now, take the remaining chapters and, in sequence, put them along the pathways between each of the points you've selected as major plot markers? Do they all fit? Are you bunching them up, like too many cans of beans along a conveyer belt? Are they spread out too far? Are they scattered all up and down the tree? Are you flinging yourself back and forth across the branches?

---

[18] *Plotto* was packaged in a nice hardback edition by Tin House a few years ago, and it's definitely an interesting book to have on your shelf. Though you almost need an advanced degree in mathematics and programming logic in order to decipher the shorthand code that link all the various plot points together.

In the process of answering these questions, have you started to see cracks in our outline? Does your plan still work, or do you need to reconsider some of the elements you've got in play?

Naturally, make changes as they become evident.

You may find that we're still working at such a high level that you're not seeing the granularity you'd like for each chapter. "Yes, but how do I get from the start of a chapter to the end?" you're wondering. As it so happens, that job falls to your characters.

CHARACTER

WE'RE GOING TO LET YOU IN ON A LITTLE SECRET: PLOT doesn't drive a book; character does. Yes, of course, a book should be a series of events that take you from point A to point B, but the circuitous route you take from A to B (past the Zoo at C, around the hedge marked D where the old lady likes to walk her toy poodle, and then down the alley behind the sandwich shop at E, et cetera) is what propels your story along. As easy as it would be to strap your characters into a trolley car and let it trundle blithely along this route, that is never going to happen. Why? Because your characters are going to want to do something different.

Damn characters.

Life is interesting because it does not follow the route we think it should take. Think back on what you were doing a year ago, or even three years ago. Are you where you thought you would be? Have you written all the books you meant to write? Have you written *any* of the books you thought you were going to write? [19]

---

[19] I know. I'm surprised by the books that come out of my head too.

When people talk about "pantsing" as writers, what they mean is: "I know better than to do a lot of pre-planning because my characters are going to take over the narrative and figure out how to solve the plot on their own." Which is still writer code for "making shit up as you go," but now you're blaming it on someone else. "I didn't plan this; the characters did!"

Sure, blame them. But let's step back for a second and look at how character happens. It might go something like this: you get up, stagger around your house for a little while, trip over the cat once or twice, and eventually get enough coffee in your bloodstream that you can put a coherent thought together. Now, you're standing in front of your closet, trying to decide what you wear. Unless you're Albert Einstein or Neil Gaiman, you have choices. Are you going to wear that shirt with the funny duck logo or the striped pants? Are you going to go with those awesome slingbacks that you've been waiting all winter to wear, or are you going to stick with the less than awesome but ultimately much warmer faux-fleece lined boots? Are you going to do something with your hair or wear a hat?

All of these decisions that have to be made before you leave the house are creating character. This costume popinjay is who you are going to be when when you leave the house. This *character* is going to interact with the world in a very distinct way (and the world will interact back in a similarly distinct way).

Whatever "plot" you imagined for the day is going to be impacted by this character you've assembled. Sure, your "character" may have been influenced by the plot you've constructed, but what if you created a "character" that was contradictory to your plot? What is going to happen? Ah, see how that works?

Now, in light of the book you are writing, how readily do your characters dress correctly for your plot?

And if they are perfectly matched, what's the conflict in your story?

Consider, for instance, Clive Cussler's long-time hero, Dirk Pitt (and now, Dirk Jr.) or Matthew Reilly's Shane Schofield. They're the best of the best of the ultra-best, and yet they continually end up in situations where they must save the WHOLE WORLD (usually by happy hour on Thursday). Once or twice, we can manage to sustain belief, but after a half-dozen times or so, its starts to stretch credibility, doesn't it? [20]

How proficient do you characters have to be? In his book *How to Write A Damn Good Novel*, James Frey talks about the concept of maximum capacity. We won't spoil all of the discussion because the whole book is worth reading, but Frey says that a character must operate at the maximum of the capacity which they have. In other words, regardless of their skill or intelligence or empathy, they must function at the peak of their efficiency as often

---

[20] It's in *Temple*, one of the early Reilly books, where the Professor Race—the stand-in for Schofield in this book—must disarm a nuclear weapon while trapping in an M4 Abrams tank that has just been shoved out the back of a cargo plane at 30,000 feet. Naturally, he survives. But where do you go from there, narratively speaking?

as possible. Why? Because a character that is lazy, indolent, or otherwise uninterested at doing the best they can is going to put your reader off.

This is not the same as potential. Characters are impaired all the time, and in fact, impairment is critical to giving your characters somewhere to go. If they are perfect and amazing at all things, then how are they going to grow and change? We like Batman, but really? He's kinda dull because he's absolutely the best at everything.[21]

Flawed characters provide for more interesting possibilities, because—even though they are functioning at the best of their current ability—they are going to fuck things up in some way that is going to raise the stakes in the book.

Sometimes your plot goes sideways because the characters just can't do what they're supposed to do, in the time allotted. Oops. Oh, look, here comes Act III. Surprise!

Take, for instance, Christopher John Francis Boone, the narrator of Mark Haddon's *The Curious Incident of the Dog in the Night-Time*. Christopher is autistic, which presents all sorts of interesting issues for the author (especially since the book is written in first person), but what makes the book so marvelous is that Christopher—while not quite of the same mental capacity of, say, a normal teenager—still manages to solve the mystery of who killed Mrs. Shears's dog. Why? Because he persists—regardless

---

[21] It doesn't matter how you dress the story up, it's one that is so trope-y that it's nigh-impossible not to turn it into a parody, which is a problem, you know?

of the disadvantages he might appear to have. And, in fact, it is because of who he is and how he sees the world that the book was such a wide success. The same story, told from the perspective of an investigating officer, would have been nothing more than a dry incident report.

Plot all you like, but leave some room for the characters to find their own way. They're going to fight you anyway, so you might as well give them some wiggle room. And by "wiggle room," we mean, let them be interesting. Let them do interesting things. Let them interact with the world in an interesting way. Because, that's what is going to make your book interesting and different.

EXERCISE

Imagine your character is being interviewed by the IRS. Imagine your character is going to be on a celebrity television show where they are going to bake sugar cookies in front of a live studio audience. Imagine your character is going to perform a high-wire act, while blindfolded! And with a penguin strapped to their chest!

In short, create an interesting scenario—something brief; it doesn't have to be complicated—and put your character in the midst of it. Let them go. Let's see what they do. And what does that tell you about who they are and what they find important?

Your characters have a say in what you're doing; you might as well listen to what they've got to say.

CHEWING ON THE SCENERY

IF A PLOT IS A SERIES OF POINTS CONNECTED BY PATHWAYS, then scenes are stones upon the pathways. Scenes, much like plot points, follow a linear progression. Even if they don't seem linear, they are—in some fashion. Books have a beginning, a middle, and an end. The arrangement of words on the page may not correspond to the beginning, middle, and the end of the story, and that's fine because writers with MFAs have to have outlets, too. Somewhere, there is a map that reads: "this happens, and then this happens, and then this happens . . ." Each word, each scene, and each plot point occurs in the only order possible for the book to have the effect the author wants on the reader's mind.[22]

We know what a plot is, and we know what words are, so what is a scene? A scene is drama, and drama, as screenwriter David Mamet once remarked in a legendary memo to the writers of the television show *The Unit*, is "the quest

---

[22] Unless you're writing hypertext or some such nonsense, in which case you're on your own. And I say that with great fondness for these sorts of constructions.

of the hero to overcome those things which prevent him from achieving a specific, acute goal."[23] A scene, Mamet goes on to explain, must answer three questions:

1) Who wants what?
2) What happens if they don't get it?
3) Why now?

WHO	**WANTS**	**WHAT**
HOW	**WHY**	**HOW**
WHAT	**WHY**	**HOW**

---

[23] http://goo.gl/W6OKyc

We can turn these questions into a series of boxes. [24]

The first line is simply a reiteration of the first question: "Who wants what?"

The second line asks "How are they going to get it? Why do they want it? And how are they going to be thwarted?"

Finally, the third line is "What is their course of action to get what they want? Why is that quest going to fail? How is it going to fail?"

This is your basic breakdown of a scene.

Each of these is boxes is a discrete component of the scene, and if you work through these row by row, you will present information to the reader in a manner that they will naturally absorb. Anytime you find yourself presenting the "WHY" on the second row before you've presented all of the first row, you're probably writing the scene backwards. You're giving us information about the scene prior to us knowing how to position it in relation to the rest of the scene.

Scenes are chunks of information, frankly, delivered in a manner that is dramatic and engaging. We have to pass a lot of information on to the readers so that they understand what is at stake in a given scene, but as soon as they spot us spoon-feeding them this data, they're going to knock the spoon out of our hands and wander off. You have to keep them interested in the spoon. You want them

---

[24] Nine, in fact, because I like that sort of symmetry. Plus it fits with stuff in APPENDIX B.

to want the spoon, and you want to give them a way to get the spoon. Does this sound familiar?

What does the person in this scene *want*?

How do they *get* it?

What do they *need* it for?

How will they *use* it?

"Chewing on the scenery" is a phrase used to describe actors who dive into their roles with such relish that they overplay the emotional content of a scene. Their angst is just shy of offing themselves with every line of dialogue, their outrage is nearly incendiary, and their despair is filled with much gnashing of teeth and tearing of the hair. They act like it's live theater at an outdoor sports arena, and they want to be sure that the kids in the cheap seats who are a half a mile away can still see the emotional *drama* of the scene. Which gets a little overwrought when an extreme close-up goes up on the Jumbotron.

But you have to think about each scene in your book with this level of intensity. It probably won't make it to the page, but ask yourself exaggerated questions about the scene as you consider it. Who will die if Person A doesn't tell Person B about the ham sandwich in the refrigerator? Will Person C be left alone *forever* if they don't confess their undying adoration for Person D in this scene? Will everyone within a hundred miles be turned into chicken nuggets if Person E doesn't figure out how to disarm the nuclear transmogrifier in less than five seconds?

Most of the time your answer will be in the negative, but in stating as much, you should be able to explain why that scene is important anyway. And if you can't, then what is that scene doing in the book? Or are your characters doing what author John Hedtke refers to as "walking the mall?"[25]

Once upon a time, Rajesh Setty wrote an article for *Lateral Action* where he talked about the six levels of engagement in online conversation.[26] People pass through fairly distinct stages in their conversations. They start with mild banalities, and then then move through successively more direct and personalized levels of interaction. Eventually, they're talking with a high degree of creative thinking.

Speaking of which, I once had a conversation with a customer in the bookstore I was working at that followed this same course. Once we reached this final stage, he informed me that we had just participated in a course of Transactional Analysis (based on work done by Eric Berne).[27] Imagine how delighted I was to have been party to a creative conversation!

Anyway, if we were to chart this conversation, it might look something like this:

i. Greeting. Initiating a conversation. *"Hi, how are you?" "I'm fine. How are you?"*

---

[25] "Walking the mall" works for Richard Linklater and David Mamet (and for Kevin Smith, to some extent). The rest of us need to have something happen on the page.

[26] http://lateralaction.com/articles/engagement-conversations/

[27] Naturally, I couldn't find an exact correlation in Berne's work, so take the source of this theory with a grain of salt.

ii. Polite discourse concerning local phenomena. *"Nice weather we're having." "Yes, it's fabulous how lemon-colored the sky is these days."*

iii. Discourse concerning the personal sphere of each individual. *"How are the kids?" "How's your health?"*

iv. Future-looking discourse. *"Any plans for the weekend?" "Still thinking about getting shot into space?"*

v. Critical inquiry and/or revelation of personal information. *"I think I'm turning into a wombat."*

vi. Reaction to revelation or response to critical inquiry. *"Wow. I didn't know about the bees living in your skull. Okay, well, gotta run!"*

In his article, Setty argues that the first three stages require little effort for creative thinking and that they aren't terribly intelligent levels of communication. Polite questions. Polite answers. Everyone is working through their mental list of questions and answers via their mental dropdown lists.[28]

Once we get to layer iv, however, we start asking questions that require some creativity, and then layer v occurs when familiarity between the parties is established, and

---

[28] And let's not forget the classic dropdown menu call and response. "Hey, buddy. You got a dead cat in there, or what?"
VISUAL EFFECT OF A COMPUTER SELECTING FROM A LIST.
CHOSEN REPONSE: "Fuck you, asshole."

we can comfortably share actual emotion-rich content. For men, this is the layer where they are prone to panic and flight. For women, this is the layer where they relax and actually communicate. Funny how we're all wired.

And then in layer vi, we have the response to the interaction in layer v.

Communication through these six layers is not unlike the structure of a scene. Who wants what? How do they get it? Are they successful, and if so, how do they use what they've received?

As the creative director of this magical gathering, you have to know the purpose of the scene. You have to know what each character wants from that conversation (and many times, what they want is not immediately relevant in the words that are coming out of their mouths).[29]

We're writing long-form fiction, which means we get a little leeway in how we present information to the readers, but each character is living in a world that is scripted not dissimilar to a film or television show. All they get is lines of dialogue. They have to figure out what the other players want from what they say and do. They don't get the luxury of third party omniscient viewpoint.

In fact, screenplay writing will—very quickly—show you whether you are writing around the dialogue or to the dialogue. Adverbs are a sure sign that you're having to

---

[29] *cf.* any scene in *Downton Abbey*, except for the scenes with the Dowager Countess of Grantham, which are as refreshing as they are bracing for their brash directness.

explain the emotional emphasis behind a line of dialogue. Pay attention to how your characters are communicating (or not) with each other, and ask yourself why they're not going to the conversational level that you want them to.

As cliché as it is, don't be afraid to ask what any character's motivation is for that—or any—scene.

PRUNING

WRITING ISN'T JUST A MATTER OF STRINGING WORDS TOGETHER. Sometimes, you have to unstring the words you've got and restring them. Or get a different string entirely. Hemingway was interested in telling a story; Joyce was interested in having a love affair with language. They're just different writers, approaching their content in different ways. Write in the style of the story that you're telling, but be succinct and to the point. Elmore Leonard's tenth tip for writers is to "leave out the parts that readers tend to skip."

I can be terrible at listening to my own advice, and I had a hard time recently with the opening to a book. Eventually, I realized the first ten pages of the book are nothing more than me nattering on about world-building. I'm just getting a feeling for the character and the world he is wandering through. The first line of the book is actually the last line of chapter one because that is where things actually start happening.

The first line of Stephen King's *The Gunslinger* is: "The man in black fled across the desert, and the gunslinger followed."

From *The Rainy City*, the first book in Earl Emerson's Thomas Black series: "On Saturday some ghoul murdered my dog."

From James Joyce's *Finnegan's Wake*: "riverrun, past Eve and Adam's, from swerve of shore to bend of bay, brings us by a commodious vicus of recirculation back to Howth Castle and Environs."

Do you see how these writers cut to the quick? Well, maybe not Joyce, but he's *recirculating* here anyway.

Now, can I remember the first line of Stephen King's *Bag of Bones*? Nope. But do I remember the ghost who grabs the protagonist from under the bed at the end of chapter one, thereby hooking me for the rest of the book? Absolutely. Would that moment have worked as well as the first line of the novel? Probably not. Pace yourself. Give the book some room to breathe, but be aware of why you are giving the book this space.

I once wrote a thriller, which was picked up by an independent genre house. One night, the publisher called (something he never did); he wanted to chat about the book. "I have some notes," he said. "Well, one note, actually. There's this section where the characters are in Santiago. It just . . . it just drags."

"I know," I said. "I had no idea what happened next, but I kept writing anyway, hoping the plot would show up. If you hadn't noticed, then it didn't need fixing, right?"

He laughed and laughed and laughed. "So, you've got this, then?"

"Yep, I got it."

He was talking about a ten-thousand word chunk in the middle. He called because he was worried that I wouldn't react well to having to rework a sizeable chunk of the story. I wasn't worried, because I already knew that not only was that section of the book a mess, but so was the fifteen thousand words leading up to it. It all needed to go, and so I cut it all, reworked the middle, and sent it back.

Ten years ago, I would have tried to rewrite the whole book, because I didn't understand the point of editing.

I used to loathe that part of the process. Now, it's the part I like best, because it is during this aspect of making a book that I get to shape this mess of words into something resembling that thing in my head. I know what kind of tree I have; now I am pruning.

Some people write thirty thousand word outlines, and then do one draft of a book and they're done. If I'm going to write that many words in an outline, I'm might as well just write the book. Honestly, though? I probably cut about 30 - 40K from a manuscript during the editing process, so it's probably the same amount of work in the end. Big Outliner is more efficient than me. Whatever. That's their process.

It's important to give yourself permission to cut. Cut dialogue. Cut scenes. Cut subplots. Cut entire character arcs. Be ruthless and mean, and learn to be efficient. Because—and it took some time for this to sink in—this is not the only book you're ever going to write. This idea is not your only idea. These lines of dialogue are not the last lines of dialogue that are every going to come out of your fingers. You are a writer. You can always write more words.

The trick, as with everything, is knowing when *not* to write.

PART THREE

STAYING THE COURSE

THE LATE NIGHT PEP TALK

We've talked about how to get your butt in the chair, and we've done some diagramming and theory about the structure of your book. Now, let's talk about the hardest part: showing up and doing the work. Day after day.

You're probably familiar with the whole "lie in bed and stare at the ceiling for an hour" experience. It's not quite insomnia, is it? Nor is it time to get up, either. It's just dark, and you're in bed, waiting for your brain to shut up. It's not like your brain is farming itself out for bitcoin calculations or 3D rendering; it's just *not quiet*.

You get up, and wander into the room with your computer and turn it on. Oh joy! It wants to update everything. You click 'yes' and then sit there for an hour—maybe two—staring at the computer screen instead of the ceiling. This is totally calming that crawling sensation of utter helplessness that is working its way under and through and all over your skin, isn't it?

The core of this unease is that you're dwelling on all the things you're supposed to be doing. Deadlines. Social engagements you couldn't weasel out of. Oh, and you're not worried about money. No. That's not part of it, at all.

Brains really suck sometimes.

Most of the time, brains are helpful, like when you're trying to figure out the best line to use when you're meeting someone you've had your eye on for some months. Or the best response to a cutting remark from a coworker, who you know is being an ass because they're terrified that they're going to be the one who is going to get cut during the next seasonal Reduction In Force. Or when trying to figure out which of the two windows at the drive-up espresso shack is going to move faster.[30]

And then there are the times when your brain is nothing more than a dark, dark well of self-doubt and despair. Especially in the middle of the night. Kind of like your bladder. It needs to be emptied regularly or it starts exerting an awkward pressure on the rest of your internal organs—a rather insistently awkward pressure. Sure, you'd rather be lying there in bed, lolling about peacefully, but oh no, not your bladder.

Wouldn't it be more efficient if you could just evaporate your pee through tiny flaps rather than having to get up, find the toilet, do your business, and stagger back to bed? You could just roll over slightly to make sure your waste vents were not being blocked and *voila!* Urine evaporation.

---

[30] Neither of which are open at 3am, by the way, when you've finally decided to quit pretending you're going to go back to sleep.

We should totally get working on this, evolutionarily speaking. Especially if this solved the problem of having doubt. Hey, just roll over, expose some brain vents, and *voila!* All our doubts turns to vapor and drift away.

A tangent, I know, and it's the sort of thing that rattles around my head when I'm staring at the ceiling. It's entertaining for a minute or two, but then the rest of the noise comes back. That's the stuff that is really bad.

I'm not writing enough.

I'm not doing enough social media.

Why am I not getting any reviews for my books?

Why do these two characters refuse to play well together?

How can I make myself look sexier to a prospective agent/ editor/publisher?

Should I wear a hat in my author photos? Does it make my head look big?

Does the cat like me?

Who am I kidding about this writing thing? They're going to spot me for being a phony as soon as I get out of bed, aren't they?

And on and on. Throw in some financial concerns and a couple dashes of relationship angst and it's almost a full-on panic. *Maybe someone I know is going to die soon!* That won't add any stress. Gosh, no!

This is what weighs on you at two in the morning—that invisible, yet persistent, weight. Making it hard to breathe. Making it hard to turn over. Making it hard to get much needed rest. It's what happens when your brain opens a dark hole and dives in, dragging you with it.

This is the deep well of doubt. We fall into the well more readily when it is dark and we can't see where we're going.[31] On occasion, we can throw some boards over the top and dance across it like we're without a care in the world, but eventually, those boards get knocked aside. The hole is still there. Big and dark. Waiting for us.

Hey, there's probably a dead fish or two down there, your brain points out. *Shouldn't we go check?*

Here's a secret: no one else can see this hole. No one else is going to accidentally fall into your well of doubt. You made it up, and you can un-make it too. If you're lying in bed at two in the morning, get up. Go sit on the toilet, take a deep breath, and let all of this fear and apprehension out. You don't have doubt vents any more than you have urine vents, and the only way to get all of this terror out of you is to forcefully—mindfully—expel it. Sit and piss it away, if you like. It's just waste that needs to be dumped. *Fear is the mindkiller*, goes the old saying,[32] and who cares if it comes from a book about some desert planet far in our future. It's still true.

Fear keeps you awake. Fear keeps you from making a choice. Fear keeps you from daring to do something different and amazing. Fear keeps you from realizing that you've got this.

---

[31] Sometimes metaphors are more real than you want them to be.

[32] One of the more memorable Bene Gesserit sayings from *Dune*, and I'm willing to bet it started out as a bit of marginalia that Frank Herbert wrote to himself as he was wondering if this whole ecological-SF-desert-world, giant-sandworms book was a good idea.

We're writers. We play the *What if?* game more often and more readily than small dogs think about breakfast. Doubt is nothing more than your brain sputtering through all the permutations and scenarios you've been throwing in your own path. Once it runs out of those, what is it going to do? It's going to get in trouble because it doesn't have anything better to do. It's absolutely responsible and forward-thinking of you to consider all the possibilities, but once you've done a round or two of mental extrapolation, stop. Move on.

As with all things in life and in fiction, once you stop endlessly circling the dark well of doubt, you'll start moving forward again. And you know what? Just as your characters experience obstacles and opportunities in their second act, so will you. Embrace them or dodge them. Be as clever as your characters. Why? Because you invented them, and anything they can do, you can do as well. Make choices that will either close doors or open new ones, because that is what you do when you climb out of the well and start moving forward.

Lying in bed at two in the morning, waiting for your bladder to fill, is floating around at the bottom of the well. Climb out, pee (if you need to), and go make something. A sandwich, a cup of tea, a blanket fort. It doesn't matter.

Don't float. Move, instead.

PARETO'S SECRET

Okay, so now we've talked ourselves into moving. But are we running or walking? Do we have the right shoes? How are we going to stay hydrated?

Well, those are good questions, but they're also getting into the minutiae again. Tell your brain to knock it off. In fact, let's do some math. That always quiets the noise.

Now, once upon a time, there was an Italian economist and philosopher who, while standing out on the back porch of his villa, surmised that there was an uneven distribution of peas in the pea pods in his garden. He may have been talking metaphorically about the state of land ownership in Italy; he may have been talking about peas. This is one of those stories where it's best to not get tied up in the minutiae. Having proposed this theory, he sent workers out into his garden and—lo and behold!—they discovered 20% of his pea pods contained 80% of the peas in the garden. This revelation became known as the Pareto Principle, or more commonly, the 80/20 rule.

20% will produce 80% (and, inversely, 80% will produce 20%), which is to say that 20% of the effort required will produce 80% of the work needed, and that remaining 20% will require 80% of the remaining effort. Basically, you can expend 20% of your energy and net yourself a B grade. Getting that A? That's a lot more work, which drifts us into the nebulous realm of ROI—return on investment. It's an acronym that data-driven business folks like to use, and we'll probably end up hating it, but let's not ditch it quite yet.

Anyway, how does the Pareto Principle apply to writing?

Well, consider the following maxim: "A good book is one that is finished." And by "finished," I mean "you have written a long string of words that ends with 'THE END.'"

We can argue whether this is a good maxim or not later, but "finishing" is 80% of the work. Polishing that book? Editing the life out of that book? You're in that remaining 20% stage, which is going to take how much work? That's right. A lot more.

Now, I'm not advocating a lack of editing. You should always edit, but recognize that a lot of the basic work of creating the book has been done already. Editing is something you can do forever, but recognize you are in the realm of diminishing returns.

Now, if your editing doesn't seem to be getting you closer to having a book that you'll let out of the house—and this is where you need to have a stern talk with yourself—then what's really wrong?

The characters are on the page. You have a plot outline. You have filled out all the fields on our master chart. The words should spill out of you, flowing faster than you can type or write. Is there something awry with the plot? Are the characters pushing back against the plan you have? Are you concerned that someone—somewhere—will take offense to your story and talk meanly about your words? Are you worried that this book won't be as "good" as your last book? Or that your book won't be as well received as a similar book written by one of your peers?

Well, these first two concerns can be addressed by taking some time and going back over your planning materials. If you don't want to write the book, there's probably a simple reason why, and it will undoubtedly have something to do with the shape of the plot or the characters. You have the power to fix that. You're the writer.

I recently had a conversation with a writer who was struggling with their book. They had a solid plot outline but didn't like the characters. They weren't engaging with the plot like they were supposed to. "Do you know which one is the protagonist?" I asked. They nodded, and I said "So, kill that person in the next chapter, and then write the rest of the book."

They didn't like that suggestion. "But what about all the words that I've done already?"

"It's just words," I said. "You can write more."

"But I . . . I like this character."

"Do you? Because if you did, they'd like you back, and you two would be playing well together. And if that is the case, then maybe that protagonist is pushing back because they're the wrong protagonist for the plot you've got."

I didn't actually think that whacking the protagonist was the solution, but I wanted to shake this writer out of the box they had trapped themselves in. I wanted to give them permission to look hard at the pieces they had collected for the book and seriously question if these pieces were really meant for this book. As the writer talked through all the pieces and the place in the plot, they would probably realize what wasn't working.

Because it is one thing to think you know what is going on, and an another thing entirely to explain it to someone else. Many a plot has been saved by trying to talk through and discovering how embarrassed you are about the plot holes you've been subconsciously skimming past.

You have to trust that you know how to write a story, and when that story isn't coming, it's because something isn't quite right in your plan. Your brain knows, and when you struggle, that's because your brain is trying to tell you where the story is broken.

As for the remaining concerns, these are completely out of your control. Theodore Sturgeon had a revelation that was later codified into a law, and it is: "Ninety percent of anything is crap."[33] This is quintuply true for commentary on the internet. The best thing you can do for your sanity, your career, and for everyone around you is to ignore what anyone says on the internet.

No good ever—EVER—came from trying to correct some jackass's misread of your work. They're just expressing their opinion, which is fine. That's what why we evolved

---

[33] It's in the OED, so it must be true.

fingers and mouths, though many should probably stick with using those fingers to shove root vegetables and rocks into their mouths, rather than attempt to communicate with electronic signals shot into the intertubes.

If you find yourself unable to step away from the keyboard, here is what I recommend:

> *- Write a reply that says: "I wrote a book, and you didn't. Hahahahaha!"*
> *- Read it out loud where no one can hear you.*
> *- Delete your reply without actually sending it.*
> *- Get on with your life.*

That sentence—"I wrote a book, and you didn't"—is all that matters, because that is what is pissing them off. They can't take that away from you, no matter how hard they try. You put your butt in your chair, and you made a book. They were busy being outraged on the Internet.

Pareto's Rule applies here, too. You're never going to make everyone happy, and it will take an inordinate amount of energy and time to convince a very small portion of the world otherwise. Twenty percent of your time and attention is good enough for eighty percent of the world.

Outrage on the Internet is fun, but you're working the wrong side of the equation if you're spending too much time there.

REACHING THE END

WE TOUCHED ON THIS BRIEFLY IN THE LAST CHAPTER, BUT let's say it again, because mantras make the world go round, right?

The definition of a good book is one that is finished.

Writing can be easy work or it can be hard work, but it is still work, nonetheless. It may look like you're not doing much when you're sitting there with your feet up on the desk, staring at the ceiling. Or when you're off vacuuming the cat for the fortieth time this week. And you certainly don't build muscles writing like you do when you're out working construction. Nor do you get any sort of decent tan.

What we do have is charts and graphs and diagrams that tell a story. All that is left to do is put some words down. Lovely, lovely words. And the only way those words are going to happen is if you put your butt in your chair and your fingers on your keyboard. Eighty percent of why you don't write is an excuse, which is fine, really, because we know that the other twenty percent is totes sweet productive time, don't we?

Heck, I just wasted the first hour of my two hour writing block this morning when I should have been working on this chapter. Why? Because I was staring at a blank page, and I didn't have a snappy anecdote to start things off (read excuse). I had a pretty good idea of what I wanted to say in this chapter, but I didn't know how I was going to say it, and so I didn't. I fiddled around the office, paid some bills, and stared out the window for a bit. And now, I've only got an hour today instead of two. I'm going to type faster in this hour to make up for not working. It's a terrible way to be productive, but it's my way, more often than not. I own it, though, and at the end of the day, I still get to put a number down in the column for today's word count. I don't bother noting how I got those words. What matters is that I got them.

We talked about units of GWT in the planning section, and how it takes many units of GWT to write a book. If you stare at that number, the project can seem impossible, so don't stare at it. Give yourself a goal you know you can hit. If you think you can get ten units in a week, put a stack of twelve counters in a box on your desk. At the end of every day, open the box and take out however many units you earned. Or put counters in an empty box. Whichever works better for you. The important point is that the box is closed when you're working so that you have no idea how many counters are in there (or not).

It's the same if you use a stopwatch timer for your GWT unit. Don't put it where you can see it counting. It's not Schrödinger's stopwatch. It's counting whether you look at it or not. Let it do its job without you hovering over it. Focus on writing and not clock-watching.

And hey, if you empty your counter box before the end of the week, put some back in and earn them out again. Give yourself a reward, though, for hitting your goal. If it is a good reward, it's worth trying to hit twice in a week.

In the video game world, this is called the "feedback loop." All modern games have many, many micro goals that stack up while you're trying to reach whatever primary goal there is for the game. Most games have between forty and a hundred million hours of gameplay built into them. If we had to play the minimum before we got any sort of reward, no one would finish a game. But there are many minor goals that can be achieved on the way. "Log in four days in a row, and get a fox hat." "Stab fifty orcs, and get double XP for the rest of the week."

These are all little things that keep you playing. "Oh, I've killed forty-two orcs today. Well, I guess I can keep playing for another hour to stab those last eight . . ."

Build feedback loops for your writing time. If you use poker chips for your counters, create goal states for the colored chips. Blues are worth five hundred words. Five blues gets you a green. Green chips can be turned in for a visit to the frozen yogurt shop. Ah, but five green chips can be turned in for a red chip, which can be redeemed for a visit to the local bookstore or a movie night.

Use the chips for the whole family. You earn a red chip, which is worth having someone else cook you dinner some night. But aha! Your partner has earned two red chips by taking care of other household chores while you've been writing, and they trump you with "What me, cook? We're going out!" reward.

Feedback loops—these micro goals—work when it is possible to earn them quickly and regularly. You should be able to earn at least one or two counters for every unit of GWT. Nothing makes your day run more smoothly than you being obnoxiously pleased with yourself for having done a productive amount of creative work. Conversely, nothing sucks the fun out of the room faster than a writer bobbing around in the well of doubt.

A writer friend of mine once struggled with getting his butt in his office chair. He liked writing; he just didn't like sitting in that room. And so, he plastered the walls of the room with centerfolds from various magazines, and shockingly! he didn't mind being in that room as much anymore.

Some writers write at a desk that faces a blank wall so that they aren't distracted. For awhile, I had to write at a noisy coffee shop with my headphones blaring loops of rhythmic noise because that was the only way I could shut everything out enough to focus on the page.[34]

Progress happens because work gets done. At the end of the day, you want to run up that special *I Made Words!* banner, so that everyone knows that you've been productive. It's not a subjective act—the raising of the banner—

---

[34] I can still write just about anywhere, but I do get fussy about a chair being too soft.

it's either up or down. Did you make words? Then the banner goes up.

Writing is writing, except when it is editing, and you can't edit anything until you've written something.

A good book is a book that is finished.

A better book is one that has been polished and released into the world.

James Joyce once took two days to finish two sentences for *Ulysses*. When asked if that time had been spending trying to find the right words, Joyce is said to have replied, "No, I have the words already. What I am seeking is the perfect order of words in the sentences I have."

No one is going to love your book as much as you do. Except when you've been through it eight times during editorial, and then, everyone is probably going to like the book more than you do.

And there will be frustrated egomaniacs who will hate your book merely because they're enraged that someone wrote something and they have to pay for the pleasure of hating it. There's not much to be done about those folks.

Many people just won't care one way or another that you wrote a book. These are all reasons for you to pre-judge your book, thereby giving yourself permission to abandon it out in the muddy field behind your house on some moonless night.

Well, if that's what you want . . .

But that's not the narrative arc you've assigned yourself, is it? What's the first part of the story of You the Writer? Identifying what you WANT. And what do you want? To go dig a hole out in a muddy field and bury your laptop or your journal or whatever thing it is that is the embodiment of your creative effort? I'm not kidding. Get a shovel. Put it in your hand and ask yourself, "Is this what I'm going to do with my work?"

There is no banner for *Buried My Novel*. And even if there was one, no one is going to drop by unexpectedly to share a bottle of decent bourbon with you if you're flying the *Buried My Novel* banner.

So, put the shovel down and pick up the keyboard again. Your neighbors want to come over and drink *with* you. They don't want to sit in their own homes and talk worriedly *about* you while drinking by themselves.

Writing is a solitary practice, but the end result enriches your community. Sure, you can tell yourself that you are writing just for you, but that only works until the book is done. At which point, you've done something for other people. And they'll appreciate it.

Well, the ones that matter will. The rest aren't worth your trouble. They're the one who show up late to parties, who don't bring anything to share, who noisily drink all your booze, and who miss the toilet when they use the bathroom. You don't really want them coming by anyway.

OCTOPODES

Let's talk about octopodes for a minute. They're cool, right? Well, other than being alien intelligences. But they can force themselves through keyholes! They can open jars from the inside! It's all those tentacles, which makes it easy for them to hold lots of pens. But lots of pens don't always mean getting more work done.[35]

We've done a lot of drawing and doodling and creating lists in the course of this book, and when you spread it all out on your desk, it can seem like you've got too much to do. It will be tempting to try to do all of the things all at once. *I can be an octopus*, you're thinking. *Eight arms. It'll be easy.*

But it won't work. Not like that. You can't do everything at once.

However, you can keep moving forward. There's not one path. There are many. That's what's the octopus metaphor is about.

---

[35] Unless you're an ambidextrous sort like Comte de St. Germain, and even then you've only got two hands.

Can't quite figure out that first paragraph? Skip to the second page. Character descriptions all wrong? Buy a fashion magazine and find pictures you like. Plaster them near your workspace. Put sticky note dialogue balloons on them. Doodle in the margins of pages where the plot is all wonky. Write the end first.

Keep moving.

Be an agile octopus. Slip through keyholes. Open jars from the inside. If you blow a scene when you're drafting the book, do what I do and write "[THIS IS ALL MESSED UP, BUT EXPLODY BITS ARE NEXT AND I LIKE THOSE, SO I'LL FIX THIS MESS LATER]."

After all, you should give yourself something to edit on the second pass, right? Otherwise, you'll think that you can draft a finished book in one pass, and that's dangerous thinking, my friend.

When I wrote on the commuter train, I worked in a such a piecemeal fashion that I ended up having the same clever conversation between two characters three times. Clearly, it was an important conversation to have, but only one of those three instances was the right one. Sure, I should have remembered what I was doing a little more readily, but instead of stopping during the drafting process to go look for the conversation, I just kept writing.

Progress happens because you show up. Regularly. If you look at the track record of bestselling authors, you'll find—more often than not—their breakout book isn't their first. Rick Riordan wrote six (or seven) mystery novels for adults before *The Lightning Thief* came out and made him a YA superstar. Suzanne Collins wrote the five books of *The Underland Chronicles* before she landed on *The Hunger Games*. Janet Evanovich wrote twelve romance novels before she landed on the Stephanie Plum character with *One For the Money*.

Keep writing. You get better because you finished a book and started another. Not because you kept rewriting the first ten pages a million times.

If you do falter or wander astray, remember all these notes and the exercises we've done together. Revisit them. See if you come up with the same scenarios for these exercises as you did the first time. What's changed in the interim? Do you know the characters better? Has the world of your novel drifted too far from where you started with it? How can you get back in sync with it?

If you feel like you've paved a road off into the wilderness and you're far—so very, very far—from where you are supposed to be, don't pull up the road and backtrack. Figure out how to correct your course back to the original plan. It's easier to create a shortcut that runs right through when you've got the beginning and the end connected.

And, in the end, that's what it is: a book is a line. It's a series of events that runs from a beginning, through a middle, to an end. It's a line—it may curve a bit and twist back on itself, but it's still a continuous line.

You get to the end by putting one foot—or one tentacle—in front of the other, over and over.

That's all it takes.

EXEUNT

Recently, I've taken to reading writing books while visiting the bathroom. Time on the throne is one of the few moments of the day when I'm not on someone else's schedule. What happens in the secret back room happens in its own time, at its own pace.[36] You might as well take a book in there with you. The nice thing about writing books is that many of them are meant to be read piecemeal.

With that in mind, I'd like to offer this final section as the "Bathroom Reading" section, AKA Bullet Points for Bowel Movements.

> * How long you write in any one sitting does not matter. Knowing your optimum writing time, and creating a schedule where you get that time on a very regular basis is all that matters.

---

[36] If you're fortunate enough (or young enough) that this isn't an issue, then you can skip this final summary. Get your butt in the chair and write already, you damn youngster!

* Someone is always writing faster than you. Conversely, someone is always writing slower than you. *"Are you writing?"* is the only question that is worth asking and answering.

* All plots grow out of a single tiny idea—the small seed you plant in rich, compost-heavy soil. How that seed grows into a tree is up to you, as is how well you tend to your tiny seedling as it grows into a broad, canopied tree.

* The people around you do not want you to fail. They want you to succeed because they like you better when you're not always tumbling down the well of doubt. They do not know what it is like to be a writer, but they are always thrilled to have one about. Teach them how to properly feed and ignore you. Build your feedback loops.

* When in doubt, move sideways. Pull a Tarot card. Use "And then, nuns with guns entered the room." The real question here is: Why has your book stopped moving forward?

* "Purpose, opposed by Obstacle, yields Conflict." This is your mantra.

* Chew on the scenery, and when it is soft and malleable, spit it out. What's left is probably what the scene is really about. Start there.

* All mythic structure is true. It's also a crutch. Use it to guide you back, and let go of it when you know where you are going.

* A good book is a finished book. Just as a writer is someone who writes. The rest is semantics.

"We write frankly and fearlessly, but then we 'modify' before we print."
—Mark Twain

APPENDIX A: EXTRA READING

Writing and the Creative Process

Austin, J. L., *How to Do Things With Words* (Harvard University Press, 1975).

Aylett, Steve, *Heart of the Original* (Unbound, 2015).

Bell, James Scott, *The Art of War for Writers* (Writer's Digest Books, 2009).

Bradbury, Ray, *Zen in the Art of Writing* (Bantam, 1992).

Chandler, Raymond, *The Simple Art of Murder* (Vintage Crime, 1988)

Cook, William Wallace, *Plotto: The Master Book of All Plots* (Tin House Books, 2011).

Currey, Mason, *Daily Rituals* (Alfred A. Knopf, 2013).

Field, Syd, Screenplay: *The Foundations of Screenwriting* (Delta, 2005).

Fish, Stanley, *How to Write a Sentence And How to Read One* (HarperCollins, 2011).

Goldberg, Natalie, *Writing Down the Bones* (Shambhala, 2005).

King, Stephen, *On Writing* (Scriber, 2010).

Le Guin, Ursula K., *Steering the Craft: A 21st-Century Guide to Sailing the Sea of Story* (Mariner Books, 1998).

Leonard, Elmore, *10 Rules of Writing* (Morrow, 2007).

Madden, David, *Revising Fiction* (Plume, 1988)

McKee, Robert, *Story: Substance, Structure, Style and the Principles of Screenwriting* (Regan Books, 1997).

Miller, Henry, *On Writing* (New Directions Publishing, 1964)

Orwell, George, *Why I Write* (Penguin Books, 2005)

Rand, Ken, *The 10% Solution* (Fairwood Press, 1998).

Rand, Ken, *From Idea to Story in 90 Seconds* (Fairwood Press, 2007).

Smiley, Jane, *13 Ways of Looking at the Novel* (Anchor Books, 2006).

Truby, John, *The Anatomy of Story: 22 Steps to Becoming a Master Storyteller* (Faber & Faber, 2008).

Vandenburgh, Jane, *Architecture of the Novel* (Counterpoint, 2010).

Wilson, Colin, *The Craft of the Novel* (Ashgrove Press, 1990).

Wood, James, *How Fiction Works* (Picador, 2008).

—, *The World Split Open* (Tin House Books, 2014).

Tarot

Anonymous, *Meditations on the Tarot* (Element, 1985).

Crowley, Aleister, *The Book of Thoth* (Samuel Weiser, 1944).

Greer, Mary K., *21 Ways to Read a Tarot Card* (Llewellyn Publications, 2006).

Jodorowsky, Alejandro & Marianne Costa, *The Way of Tarot* (Destiny Books, 2009).

Katz, Marcus, *Tarosophy* (Salamander and Sons, 2011).

Kenner, Corrine, *Tarot for Writers* (Llewellyn Publications, 2009).

Papus, *The Tarot of the Bohemians* (Arcanum Books, 1962).

Pollack, Rachel, *Seventy-Eight Degrees of Wisdom* (Weiser, 2007).

Pollack, Rachel, *Tarot Wisdom* (Llewellyn Publications, 2011).

Vogler, Christopher, *The Writer's Journey* (Michael Weise Productions, 1992).

Waite, Arthur Edward, *The Pictorial Key to the Tarot* (William Rider and Son, 1911).

Yuknavitch, Lidia, *The Misfit's Manifesto* (TED Books, 2017).

Mythology

Campbell, Joseph, *The Hero With a Thousand Faces* (New World Library, 2008).

Campbell, Joseph, *The Masks of God* [in four volumes] (Penguin, 1991).

Eliade, Mircea, *The Myth of the Eternal Return* (Princeton University Press, 2005).

Eliade, Mircea, *The Sacred and the Profane* (Harcourt Brace Jovanovich, 2007).

Jung, Carl Gustav, *Four Archetypes* (Princeton University Press, 1970).

APPENDIX B: CHARTS & BOXES & STUFF

During the course of this book, we've talked about a few things that came out of *Jumpstart Your Novel*, and we've talked about the Nine Box Model, which is a methodology I use for more than just outlining. We'll start with the Nine Box, and follow it with charts & boxes & stuff. You should feel free to use these as you see fit.

NINE BOX

This is a very brief overview of the Nine Box as used for outlining. If you'd like more detail on this, naturally, I'll direct you to *Jumpstart Your Novel*. Basically, though, it works like this:

We start with the Protagonist. Who is involved in something that Hooks our attention. Which reveals the Adversary. [This is the first row.]

These three boxes provide enough framework for the author to articulate the Goal of the Protagonist. In order to achieve this Goal, the Protagonist suffers a series of Obstacles and Opportunities. [This is the second row.]

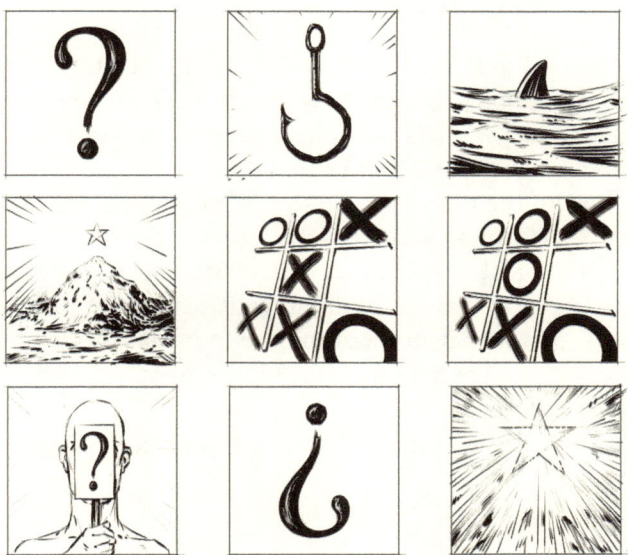

For the final row, we consider what the authorial vision is for this book, which provides a framework to consider the Change the Protagonist undergoes during the course of the novel. And, finally, how does that Change get represented on the page while still completing the author's goal? Does everyone ride off into the sunset? Is life just a field of daisies? Does everything go boom before fading to black?

Who knows, but it all leads to this final resolution.

THE BIG OUTLINE CHART

It's good to know the natural rhythms and structure of story. You don't have to slavishly adhere to every stage of every model, but it is valuable to know the stages and pace through which most stories go.

Most of the time I use these markers to help me figure out when a book isn't working. When I map the outline into this grid, I usually see that I'm skipping steps or that I have things out of order, which is creating tension that I may or may not wait to have in my book. Or I may discover that I'm missing something entirely, which is why the book feels off.

It's a guide. It's not a set of rules. Treat it accordingly.

CHAPTER	BOX	3-ACT	LESTER DENT	CAMPBELL	TAROT
1	BOX 1	ACT 1	Heap of Trouble	The Call to Adventure	THE HEART
2	BOX 2			Refusal of the Call	THE IMMEDIATE FUTURE
3				Supernatural Aid	
4	BOX 3			The Crossing of the First Threshold	THE OPPOSING FACTOR
5				The Belly of the Whale	
6	BOX 4	ACT 2	More Trouble	The Road of Trials	THE VISION
7				Meeting the Goddess	
8	BOX 5			Woman as Temptress	THE GUIDE
9				Atonement with the Father	
10				Apotheosis	
11	BOX 6		Still More Trouble	The Ultimate Boon	
12				Refusal of Return	
13				The Magic Flight	
14	BOX 7	ACT 3	Resolution	Rescue from Without	THE MIRROR
15				Crossing the Return Threshold	
16	BOX 8			Master of Two Worlds	THE EYE
17				Freedom to Live	
18	BOX 9				THE OUTCOME

THE NINE BOX PLANNER

I use a modified Nine Box layout for my daily planner. The basic premise is that I break down projects into slices that can readily fit in one unit of GWT (Glorious Writing Time), and I put each of those in one of the boxes of the upper group. I usually use the first row for "Things That Must Be Done Today," the second for "Things That It Would Be Nice To Get Done," and the last for "Things That Probably Won't Happen, But Gee, It Would Be Nice If They Did."

Naturally, you can see how this leads to many days with not many boxes crossed off.

The point being: you can't do two things at once, and if you are like me and have a gazillion projects, fretting about everything means nothing gets done. But once things are put in boxes and I adhere to the first rule of working the boxes—you only can work on the thing in the box during the allocated time—I end up actually getting things done.

The secondary set of boxes is either for activities and pieces of projects that aren't critical to "business," or if I do end up putting something in the upper layer that is going to take more than an unit of GWT, then I break it down into smaller chunks.

For example: "Get groceries," "Wash car," and "Vacuum Cat" are all activities that I would put in the lower six boxes. Or if I put "Fix this f*cking book" in the upper left corner, I might break that out into "Fix the plot hole in

jan • feb • mar • apr • may • june • july • aug • sept • oct • nov • dec
1•2•3•4•5•6•7•8•9•10•11•12•13•14•15•16•17•18•19•20•21•22•23•24•25•26•27•28•29•30•31

the call to action

self check

☆

events

☆☆

fill in the dots

NOTES

teppobox.com

the nine box planner

Chapter 1," "Do that research you've been putting off," and "Figure out the antagonist's motivation for the final third of the book." Now that bigger project has been quantified into workable pieces, and what seemed like a project that was never going to get crossed off is now a matter of doing three distinct things.

The rest of the sheet is filled with markers and notes that I find useful. I always start the day with a one-line note about the plan for the day. What am I hoping to accomplish? What is my mood like? What's the weather going to be like? Is there a quote I read recently that is pertinent to what I'm working on?

The self-check boxes are for making notes about self-care, frankly. Am I drinking enough water? Check a box for each time I empty my water bottle. Am I getting up from my desk often enough? Check.

The fill-in-the-dots boxes are for doodling, because, you know, doodling happens. The notes section is for more *literary* doodling, aka Shit I Need to Write Down Somewhere So I Don't Loose Track of It.

REWARD COUPONS

In keeping with the idea of poker chips and rewards for everyone else leaving you alone during GWT, don't forget to make yourself some reward coupons too. Incremental rewards and feedback loops keep everyone invested.

I made up a little coupon book that tracks along with the course of writing a novel draft. It starts with rewarding

me for making words, and moves on to bigger rewards like more cake or booze or a visit to the bookstore. Eventually, I earn the final coupon, which is finishing the draft. Now that's a prize worth earning.

WRITER BINGO

You can also build yourself a bingo card. Use this one or make up one of your own. Put it on the refrigerator and mark off the squares as you earn them. Naturally, this bingo card is only 3 x 3, because, you know, Nine Box Model, but you can certainly make something that is more akin to the traditionally 5 x 5 bingo grid.

"Hunt Your Weasels" is, of course, a call to hunt those weasel words—words that take up space but which don't carry their own weight.

Drop 'em down the well of despair. See if you can fill that hole up.

WRITE Five Days in a Row	Deconstruct a Scene From A Favorite Book	FREE If You Talked About Writing Today
Take A Day Off From Being Afraid of Writing Crap	WRITE Something! Anything! Make words!	Hunt Your Weasels
FINISH What's the definition of a good book?	Invert Your Excuses Into a Manifesto	FREE But only if you wrote today.

ACKNOWLEDGMENTS

Grateful tip of the hat to the gang who showed up for my Clarion West One-Day Workshop where some of the material for this book was tested. I drew on a white board for a few hours, and they took notes like it made some semblance of sense. Hopefully, I managed to get all the words in the right order this time around.

Thanks also to Guy Windsor for using the phrase "mystic shit" once upon a time in reference to something else entirely, but I think he'd approve of its use herein.

Extra whiskey rations for both Erica Sage and Evelyn Nicholas, who dealt with writer panics as they should be dealt with, which is to say they parroted back the same pithy aphorisms I had said to them at some point during the last six months.

It's cute the first few times; after that, it's kind of annoying to realize you're not listening to your own advice. Good thing they're polite about reminding me.

ABOUT THE AUTHOR

Mark Teppo is the author of more than a dozen novels, ranging across a number of genres. He lives in the Pacific Northwest, where he shuffles books around on shelves in an endless effort to find more space.

You can find him online at markteppo.com.

Please sign up for his mailing list. There is free content, advance notice of new projects, and the sporadic email about otters and moose.

http://www.markteppo.com/mailing-list

LEAVING FEEDBACK

IF YOU'VE FOUND THIS BOOK TO BE USEFUL, PLEASE LEAVE A review at your favorite online venue (Goodreads, Shelfari, Amazon, Barnes & Noble, et cetera). Reviews and stars mean a lot to independent writers as they are the metric by which they are judged by the all-mighty and all-knowing algorithm. While buying a second copy of this book and giving it to a friend is a delightful and welcome reaction to the words herein, leaving a review and a rating is also greatly appreciated.

Stars = Love.

Shameless, I know. But it's what makes the world go 'round these days.

We can be rebels when it comes to our punctuation, but let's play the game when it comes to showing the love for authors.

And I'm not asking just for myself. Go give some stars to someone else whose book you've loved. Do it. I know it'll feel good.

www.ingramcontent.com/pod-product-compliance
Lightning Source LLC
Chambersburg PA
CBHW060531080526
44586CB00012B/699